KEYSTONE TOMBSTONES

BIOGRAPHIES OF FAMOUS PEOPLE BURIED IN PENNSYLVANIA

VOLUME FOUR

JOE FARRELL, JOE FARLEY, AND LAWRENCE KNORR

SUNBURY PRESS

Mechanicsburg, PA USA

Published by Sunbury Press, Inc.
Mechanicsburg, Pennsylvania

SUNBURY
PRESS
www.sunburypress.com

For information about special discounts for bulk purchases, please contact Sunbury Press Orders Dept. at (855) 338-8359 or orders@sunburypress.com.

To request one of our authors for speaking engagements or book signings, please contact Sunbury Press Publicity Dept. at publicity@sunburypress.com.

FIRST SUNBURY PRESS EDITION: August 2020

Set in Adobe Garamond | Interior design by Crystal Devine | Cover by Lawrence Knorr | Edited by the authors.

Publisher's Cataloging-in-Publication Data
Names: Farrell, Joe, author | Farley, Joe, author | Knorr, Lawrence, author.
Title: Keystone tombstones volume four : biographies of famous people buried in pennsylvania / Joe Farrell, Joe Farley, and Lawrence Knorr.
Description: First trade paperback edition. | Mechanicsburg, PA : Sunbury Press, 2020. | Includes biographical references and index.
Summary: Joe Farrell, joe farley, and lawrence knorr write about famous and infamous people buried in pennsylvania after visiting their graves.
Identifiers: ISBN 978-1-620062-96-8 (softcover).
Subjects: BISAC: BIOGRAPHY & AUTOBIOGRAPHY / Rich & Famous. | HISTORY / US History / Mid-Atlantic.

Product of the United States of America
0 1 1 2 3 5 8 13 21 34 55

Continue the Enlightenment!

And, when he shall die,
Take him and cut him out in little stars,
And he will make the face of Heaven so fine
That all the world will be in love with night
And pay no worship to the garish sun.

—William Shakespeare

Contents

Acknowledgments

The authors would first like to thank our wives. These fine ladies have all suffered through some lonely hours and days when their husbands were off trudging through cemeteries in distant towns, counties, and even states. Of course, we'd like to think they suffered. Perhaps they actually enjoyed the time we were away, in which case, we acknowledge them anyway for the warm welcome received when we returned.

We'd like to thank two Jimmy Farleys. Joe's brother took the photo of Chuck Bednarik's grave. Joe's son found the grave of Billy Heath after he couldn't locate it on a previous visit. He also took the picture of the Heath grave. Ah, the powers of youth!

We'd also like to thank Crystal Devine, our book designer, for the wonderful job done formatting this book and all of the other books in our series. Crystal was always patiently at the ready to make whatever last-minute changes that were necessary.

For this volume specifically, we'd like to thank the following un-named people:

- The groundskeeper at Union Hill Cemetery in Kennett Square. He was very helpful in finding Linda Darnell's grave. While doing so, he asked us if we were also interested in a baseball player by the name of Herb Pennock. We all looked at each other and realized we completely missed the fact the Hall of Famer was buried here, too! Of course, we accepted his help. On the way to our next stop, we unanimously decided to add Pennock to this book.

- The cemetery manager at Monongahela Cemetery near Donora. Lawrence went in to talk to him and did not come out. The Joes worried that something happened and went to investigate, only to find their teammate had acquired a stack of death certificates and grave photos. This gentleman was most helpful with the Donora Smog chapter.

- The young lady from the office at Alto-Reste Burial Park near Altoona. Again, Lawrence went in to talk to the people in the office. Again, he was taking longer than expected while the Joes waited outside. Just when they were about to give up, Lawrence exited with the young lady who guided us to the location of the grave of Betty James, saving potentially many minutes of fruitless searching. She also reminded Lawrence he had left his camera on the roof of his car and was about to drive off. This avoided the potential loss of a piece of equipment worth over $1000.

- To the grasscutter at Greenwood Cemetery near Pittsburgh. We were lost trying to find August Wilson. Thanks to his help, we were able to locate the grave of the late playwright.

- To the staff at West Laurel Hill Cemetery in Philadelphia. This is one place we did not want to leave! We were provided with snacks and drinks in a palatial waiting area. The staff then helped us locate Hy Lit's grave very quickly.

In addition, we'd like to thank author John Moore of Northumberland, Pennsylvania, who provided access to the Northumberland County Historical Society to see early artifacts related to Sunbury and for joining Lawrence on a trip in the area to find Shikellamy Town and to visit Shikellamy's grave. He also provided anecdotes about his former neighbor, Dutch Van Kirk, and his former interviewee, James McCord.

Lastly, we'd like to thank former Lieutenant Governor of Pennsylvania Mark Singel for his input regarding Budd Dwyer.

Introduction

Welcome to *Keystone Tombstones Volume 4*. Little did Joe Farley and I expect in 2011 that our idea of writing mini-biographies and visiting graves of interesting people would lead to us collaborating and publishing over twenty volumes. In addition to the four volumes of Keystone Tombstones are special editions of *Keystone Tombstones Civil War, Keystone Tombstones Gettysburg, Keystone Tombstones Sports,* and *Best of Keystone Tombstones* plus four regional Keystone Tombstones compilations.

We also have published a so far two-volume series of Gotham Graves featuring fascinating people buried in the New York Metropolitan area and one volume of Murders, Massacres, and Mayhem in the Mid-Atlantic. We are presently hard at work on a series of books about the lives and burial sites of our country's founders. We have so far published two volumes: *Graves of Our Founders Volume 1* and *Pennsylvania Patriots.* We anticipate more volumes in that series. Along the way, we acquired another partner, the multi-talented Lawrence Knorr. Lawrence's knowledge, experience, and enthusiasm have added immensely to our efforts, first as our publisher, photographer, and chauffeur, and now as a co-author. Lawrence is currently working on his Ph.D. in history.

Volume Four contains a diverse collection of interesting stories. Some subjects are well known and some not so much. Arnold Palmer, "The King," is perhaps the best known and one the best golfers of all time. Chuck Bednarik and Herb Pennock are Hall of Famers in football and baseball, respectively.

The science world is represented by Margaret Mead, Joseph Priestley, and Fred Taylor, all of whom made considerable contributions to their field of study and the world.

The entertainment world brings us the stories of the amazing triumphs of one of America's greatest playwrights August Wilson, and the incredible success of the singer, actress Pearl Bailey as well as the tragic stories of rock star Sid Vicious, Hollywood beauty Linda Darnell, and the woman many consider to be the first supermodel, Gia Carangi.

Our usual inclusion of a disaster or two is represented by the unusual story of the Donora Smog Victims, the Darr Mine Disaster, the Rhoads Opera House Fire, and the horrible Enoch Brown School Massacre.

Think Alexander Graham Bell invented the telephone? Read the chapter on Daniel Drawbaugh, and you may feel differently.

Volume Four also contains chapters on Ted Van Kirk, the navigator of the *Enola Gay*, Watergate figure James McCord, and the public suicide of Pennsylvania Senator Bud Dwyer, who many believe was innocent of the charges against him.

In the six years that have passed since the publication of *Volume Three*, fans of the series have contacted us with suggestions on who to include in any future volumes. We thank them for their interest in the series and hope this volume serves as a more than satisfying answer to their suggestions. In our view, these are fascinating stories that deserve telling. We learned a lot in writing them and enjoyed paying our respects during our visits to the gravesites. We hope you enjoy reading these stories as much as we enjoyed putting this volume together.

I.

PEARL BAILEY

"Pearley Mae"

County: Chester • Town: West Chester
Buried at Rolling Green Memorial Park
1008 West Chester Pike

Pearl Bailey was an American actress and singer. She may be best known for her role as matchmaker Dolly Gallagher Levi in David Merrick's production of *Hello Dolly* on Broadway. That performance brought her a Tony Award. She won a Daytime Emmy for her performance as a fairy godmother in the ABC After School Special, *Cindy Eller: A Modern Fairy Tale*. She received the Screen Actors Guild Life Achievement Award in 1976 and the Presidential Medal of Freedom in 1988.

Pearl Mae Bailey was born on March 29, 1918, in Newport News, Virginia, the youngest of four children of black and Creek Indian ancestry. She had no formal music education but attributed her love of song and dance to her childhood experience in a Pentecostal "holy roller" church where her father was the preacher. She began singing and dancing in her father's church when she was just three. Her parents were divorced when she was a child, and her mother remarried and moved with the children to Philadelphia. Young Pearl originally wanted to be a teacher but quit high school at fifteen.

Pearl's older brother Bill Bailey was a dancing protégé of the legendary Bill "Bojangles" Robinson (see *Gotham Graves Volume 2*, chapter 18) and had already made a name for himself when Pearl decided to enter a talent contest at the Pearl Theater where he was appearing. She won the five-dollar prize and a two-week engagement for thirty-five dollars per week. The theater closed during her engagement, and she never got paid.

Pearl Bailey

She won another contest that summer in Washington, D.C., and then after winning a competition at Harlem's Apollo Theater, she decided to quit school and pursue a career in entertainment.

Bailey began by singing and dancing in Philadelphia's black night-clubs in the 1930s and then honed her talent in the vaudeville theaters of Scranton, Wilkes-Barre, Pottsville, and other Pennsylvania coal towns. For several winters, she worked those towns for fifteen dollars a week plus tips. Then one summer on a visit to Washington, she devised a dance act that won a twelve-dollar prize and led to other engagements in Baltimore and Washington, D.C.

During World War II, Bailey toured the country with the USO, performing for American troops. That association with the USO would last her lifetime. After the tour, she settled in New York and made her first New York appearance at the Village Vanguard. She sang briefly with The Sunset Royal Orchestra and with Count Basie's band, and then for two years with Cootie William's band.

In 1944, she got a big break when the Village Vanguard booked her as a solo performer. More importantly, the club's owner suggested that she loosen up and be herself onstage. That advice helped her to create a signature style—easy and personal—engaging more with the audience between songs and even during songs. She developed a particular way of styling a song with a flavor of jazz and often some worldly-wise aside on the music's sentiment. Her popularity soared. A two-week booking at the prestigious New York supper club The Blue Angel turned into an eight-month stand, a contract with Columbia Records, and a theater tour with Cab Calloway's Orchestra. In 1945 she signed on with Cab Calloway and worked twenty weeks with him at The Zanzibar nightclub on Broadway and forged a friendship with him that would endure for decades.

In 1946 she became a Broadway sensation when lyricist Johnny Mercer and composer Harold Arlen tapped her for their all-black musical *St. Louis Woman*. Her two numbers, "A Woman's Prerogative" and "Legalize My Name," were considered the highlights of the show and Bailey received the 1946 Donaldson Award as best Newcomer on Broadway.

There is some uncertainty about the number of times Bailey married, but the last marriage to accomplished Jazz drummer Louie Belson in 1952 lasted nearly forty years until her death. The couple adopted two children.

After that, Bailey kept busy with a steady round of nightclub appearances, stage and screen performances, records, and movies. She appeared in both significant all-black musical films of the 1950s: *Carmen Jones*, co-starring Harry Belafonte in 1954; and *Porgy and Bess*, with Sidney Poitier and Sammy Davis Jr. in 1959. She won a big following with her performances of the songs "Birth of the Blues," "Bill Bailey Won't You

Please Come Home," "Let's Do It," "Come Rain or Come Shine" and "St. Louis Blues." Audiences loved her humorous and folksy style, and she was affectionately called "Pearley Mae" by her fans and close friends. In 1957 she was a featured entertainer at the Inauguration of President Eisenhower.

From the late 50s to the early 70s, Bailey regularly appeared on *The Ed Sullivan Show*, *The Perry Como Show*, and other variety programs.

Then in 1967 came the high point of her career. Bailey and Cab Calloway headlined an all-black cast version of *Hello Dolly!* The touring version was so successful that producer David Merrick took it to Broadway, where it played to sold out houses. She received unanimous raves for her work and was presented with a special Tony Award. The show ran for two years before it was forced to close due to Bailey's ongoing heart problems. During the show's run in 1968, she was awarded the Bronze Medallion; the highest award conferred on civilians by New York City. A passionate New York Mets fan, she sang the National Anthem at Shea Stadium before Game Five of the 1969 World Series. She would also sing the National Anthem before Game One of the 1981 World Series at Yankee Stadium.

In 1971, Bailey starred in her own television show. *The Pearl Bailey Show* lasted only one season, but she made numerous guest appearances on other variety and dramatic shows. For several years in the 1980s, she portrayed Lulu Baker in the situation comedy *Silver Spoons*.

In 1975 Pearl Bailey was appointed Special Ambassador to the United Nations by President Gerald Ford. As part of her role, she visited and performed for a wide variety of world leaders. She not only performed at events but on a least one occasion, she addressed a special session of the United Nations. In October 1975, she was invited by Betty Ford to sing for the Egyptian President Anwar Sadat at a White House state dinner as part of a Middle East peace initiative.

In 1978 Pearl Bailey was given an honorary degree by Georgetown University. While receiving her award onstage, she stunned and delighted her audience by announcing that she planned to return to Georgetown the following year and study for a degree. In 1985 after five years of attending classes, she graduated with a B.A. in Theology. She was 67 years old. At first, Bailey majored in French, and when asked why she switched to Theology, she said, "Because it's easier to know the Lord than it is to know French."

She wrote six books and won many awards in her lifetime, perhaps highlighted by the Presidential Medal of Freedom, awarded to her by President Ronald Reagan in 1988.

Bailey had suffered from heart trouble as early as the 1960s, but she seemed in good health in the summer of 1990 when she traveled to Philadelphia for knee surgery. She was recuperating from the operation when she died unexpectedly on August 17 at Thomas Jefferson University Hospital after collapsing in her hotel room.

She is buried at Rolling Green Memorial Park in West Chester, Pennsylvania. There is a historical marker at 1946 N. 23rd Street in Philadelphia outside the house where she lived as a youth.

Pearl Bailey's grave

2.

CHUCK BEDNARIK

"Concrete Charlie"

County: Lehigh • Town: Coopersburg
Bruied at Saint Joseph Calvary Cemetery
5203 Saint Josephs Road

Chuck "Concrete Charlie" Bednarik was a Hall of Fame center and line-backer for the Philadelphia Eagles. He was one of the last NFL players to commonly play on both offense and defense and a legendary football tough guy and was the last player in league history to regularly partici-pate in every play of an NFL game. He was known as one of the most devastating tacklers in the history of football. He played for the Eagles from 1949 to 1962 and was a key contributor to the team's NFL cham-pionships in 1949 and 1960.

Charles Philip Bednarik was born on May 1, 1925, in Bethlehem, Pennsylvania. His father, an immigrant from Czechoslovakia, was a la-borer for Bethlehem Steel. Chuck began playing football at Bethlehem's Liberty High School. Shortly after graduating, he enlisted in what was then known as the Army Air Force to fight in World War II. He became an eighteen-year-old waist gunner with the 467th Bomb Group in a B-24 Liberator. Waist gunners were charged with defending the Liberator's vulnerable sides through the use of a single machine gun. He flew on thirty combat missions over Germany for which he was awarded the Air Medal with four Oak Leaf Clusters, the European-African-Middle Eastern Campaign Medal with four Battle Stars. His last mission was on April 23, 1945, over the city of Zweisel. When he got back to England, he got out and kissed the plane, kissed the ground, and announced that

Chuck Bednarik

he was never going to fly again. Years later, Bednarik would say, "That was pressure . . . all that anti-aircraft fire they threw at us and being a nineteen-year-old kid. That gave me some toughness. So, when I survived the war and came home and went out on a football field, I figured shoot, this is easy."

He began his career at the University of Pennsylvania as a freshman late in 1945. In November of 1946, he played all sixty minutes and intercepted two passes in a 34–7 loss to unbeaten Army. He excelled as both a center and linebacker as well as punted. He was an All-American in 1947 and again in 1948 when he finished third in the balloting for the Heisman Trophy, awarded to football's leading player. Doak Walker won it that year as a junior running back at SMU. Also, in 1948 he became the first offensive lineman to win the Maxwell Award as college football's most outstanding player.

In the 1949 NFL draft, Chuck Bednarik was the first overall selection that went to the Philadelphia Eagles. After watching the first two games of his rookie season from the bench, he began a streak of "iron man" play that saw him miss just one more game over the remainder of his fourteen seasons in the league. He became a standout on both sides of the ball, earning All-Pro honors at both center and linebacker throughout his career but became most famous for his hard-hitting plays on defense. Bednarik was a member of the Eagles championship teams in 1949 and 1960.

As a player, Bednarik will always be remembered for two plays, both of which occurred in the 1960 season. In a November game against the New York Giants, Bednarik tackled running back Frank Gifford so hard he lost consciousness and was unable to return to football until 1962 and then as a wide receiver. The tackle also caused a fumble that the Eagles recovered to seal the game. The photo of Bednarik exulting alongside a prone Gifford became one of pro football's most famous images. It was perceived by some as cruel taunting. Bednarik later maintained he was unaware that Gifford was seriously hurt, claiming he was celebrating because of the fumble that sealed the win. He sent a basket of fruit to Gifford in the hospital.

Bednarik's other memorable tackle came in the 1960 Championship Game. The Eagles had a 17–13 lead over the Green Bay Packers in the final seconds of the game. Jim Taylor, the Packer fullback, broke through the line and was headed for the end zone when Bednarik tackled him at the eight-yard line and remained on top of him until time ran out, sealing the championship for Philadelphia. "You can get up now, Jim, this game is over," Bednarik told Taylor. He had played every play except the Eagles' kickoffs at the age of 35.

Bednarik was given the nickname "Concrete Charlie" by sportswriter Hugh Brown but contrary to popular belief not because of the way he played. It originated from his off-season career as a concrete salesman for

Bednarik standing over an unconscious Frank Gifford

the Warner Company. He retired in 1962 after two NFL championships, eight Pro-Bowls, and ten times elected All-Pro.

Bednarik was enshrined in the Pro Football Hall of Fame in 1967, his first year of eligibility, and the College Football Hall of Fame in 1969. Fiercely proud of his "60 Minute Man" persona, he was famously dismissive of modern players who claimed to play both sides of the ball. He was the last to play both ways until Deion Sanders did so for Dallas in 1996. Sanders especially earned Bednarik's ire. "The positions I played, every play I was making contact, not like Deion Sanders, he couldn't tackle my wife. He's back there dancing instead of hitting." His gnarled fingers stood as a reminder of his ruggedness, and he said he never made more than $27,000 in a season. At one point, he pawned his championship and Hall of Fame rings.

His uniform number 60 was retired by the Eagles in 1987, and he was named to their Honor Roll. In 1976 he returned to the Eagles as an assistant coach for Dick Vermeil. He coached until 1982. In 1999, he was ranked number 54 on *The Sporting News* list of the 100 greatest football players. In 2010 he was ranked 35th on the NFL Network's Top 100. Ironically ranked one spot ahead of him at 34 was Deion Sanders.

Chuck Bednarik's grave

Additionally, he is a member of both the Pennsylvania and Philadelphia Sports Halls of Fame.

When the Eagles chose their 75th-anniversary team in September 2007, he was honored as the best center and middle linebacker in the team's history in a ceremony at Lincoln Financial Field. The moment transcended football. "On that day," he said, "I felt like Benjamin Franklin."

Since 1995 the Chuck Bednarik Award has been given to college football's best defensive player by the Maxwell Football Club. Bednarik also served for over three decades on the Pennsylvania State Athletic Commission, which oversees boxing and wrestling in the state.

Bednarik died on March 21, 2015, after having fallen ill the previous day. He was 89. Although the Philadelphia Eagles released a statement saying he died after a "brief illness," Bednarik's daughter, Charlene Thomas, disputed that claim. She said he had Alzheimer's disease, had been suffering from dementia for years, and football-related injuries played a role in his decline. "It was not brief."

Chuck "Concrete Charlie" Bednarik is buried in St. Joseph Calvary Cemetery in Limeport, Pennsylvania.

3.

EDWARD BRADDOCK

"An Ill-Fated Expedition"

County: Washington • Town: Farmington
Buried at Fort Necessity National Battlefield
1 Washington Parkway

Edward Braddock was a British army officer who rose through the ranks in the early to mid-1700s to ultimately become the commander-in-chief for the thirteen American colonies during the French and Indian War, also known as the Seven Years' War. He and his army cut a road through the wilderness from Alexandria, Virginia, to Fort Duquesne, modern-day Pittsburgh, Pennsylvania. Their goal was to capture the French fort and assert British control over western Pennsylvania. Like the Roman legions in the Teutoberg Forest, and later Arthur St. Clair's army at the Wabash River and Custer's troops at Little Big Horn, Braddock's army was annihilated by indigenous forces. Like Varus and Custer, Braddock was mortally wounded in the battle. One of Braddock's surviving lieutenants, a Virginian provincial named George Washington, learned many lessons that would later help him during the American Revolution.

Edward Braddock was born during January 1695, in Perthshire, Scotland, the son of Major General Edward Braddock of the Coldstream Guards and his wife. The younger Braddock followed in his father's footsteps and was appointed an ensign in his father's regiment on October 11, 1710, then only fifteen. By age twenty-one, he was a lieutenant of the grenadiers. Two years later, on May 26, 1718, he fought a duel of swords and pistols in London's Hyde Park with a Colonel Waller. Both men were in the Coldstream Guards.

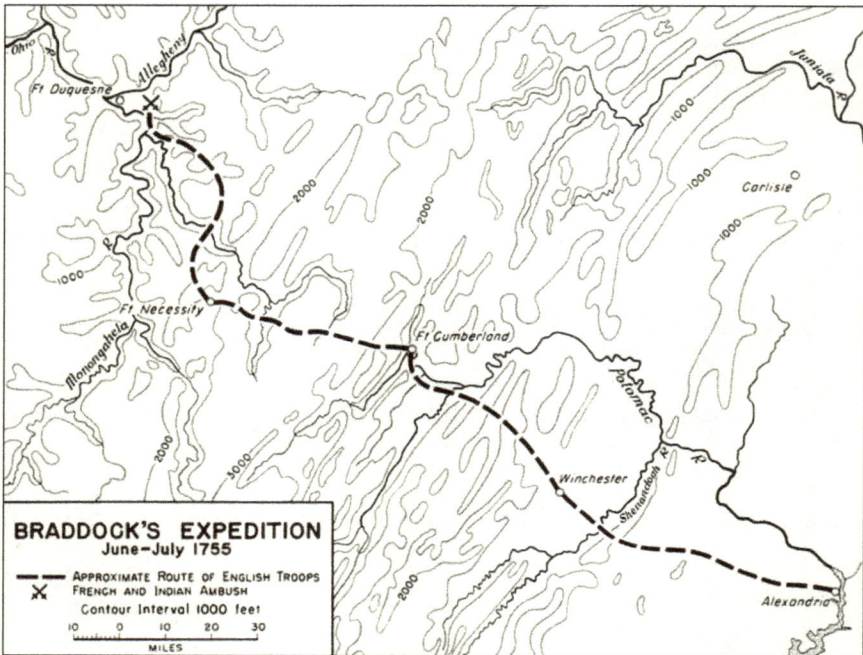

The path of Braddock's Expedition in 1755

The elder Braddock passed in 1725, but this did not deter the younger Braddock's advancement. By 1736, he was a captain and seven years later, a major. He was promoted to lieutenant-colonel of the regiment on November 21, 1745. In 1747, he fought in the Netherlands at the Siege of Bergen op Zoom during the War of the Austrian Succession. On February 17, 1753, Braddock was appointed colonel of the 14th Regiment of Foot. He was promoted to major-general the following year.

Following the War of the Austrian Succession, in 1748, there were still disputed territories in the New World, including the territory in western Pennsylvania, known as the Ohio Country. The French and the British colonies of Pennsylvania and Virginia all laid claim to it, in addition to the native tribes in the area. The ongoing negotiations between the British colonies and the natives facilitated by Conrad Weiser and his good friend chief Shikellamy had kept the peace for over twenty years. Now, with Shikellamy's passing in December of that year, negotiations became more difficult for all parties, and Weiser began fading from the scene.

In 1754, Governor Dunwiddie of Virginia, ordered a young officer, lieutenant colonel George Washington, whose brother Lawrence was a member of the Ohio Company and had land claims in the area, to lead a force into what is now western Pennsylvania to ward off the French. Hostilities broke out at the Battle of Jumonville Glen between Washington's corps and the French in late May. Washington and his men fell back and established Fort Necessity, only to surrender it shortly after that, in early July. Washington and his remaining men were permitted to abandon the fort and return to Virginia.

The following year, in response to calls from the colonies for military help, the British appointed General Braddock to commander of all forces in North America, and sent him and two regiments, the 44th and 48th, to Virginia, landing on February 20, 1755, at Hampton. The king anticipated that the colonists would unite under Braddock's leadership, but it never materialized.

Braddock was about sixty, a short, stout, bad-tempered disciplinarian with little experience in action and none of the type of fighting that was in store for him. His rudeness and arrogance made a poor impression on the colonials. George Washington, seeking a position with the British regular army, wrote to Braddock. Realizing Washington had valuable knowledge of the area, Braddock made Washington his aid as a volunteer officer. Washington privately recorded that much of Braddock's soldiers' experience had consisted of parade ground close-order drills and later described their battle performance as 'dastardly behavior.'

At a meeting with the colonial governors of Virginia, Massachusetts, Maryland, and Pennsylvania at Alexandria on April 14, Braddock was persuaded to attack the French. But, put-off by Braddock's forcefulness, some governors bristled at his demands to pay his army's expenses. The pacifist Quakers rejected his demands for money and men, even though the conflict was on their colony's western frontier. Braddock nonetheless prepared to launch his expedition from Will's Creek and Fort Cumberland in western Virginia. It was agreed that he would lead the advance against Fort Duquesne while others attacked Fort Niagara, Fort Saint-Frédéric at Crown Point, and Fort Beausejour on the Bay of Fundy.

Braddock's wounding at the Battle of Monongahela 9-July-1755

Braddock's preparations were slow and hampered by a lack of resources and administrative issues. In May, Braddock met with Benjamin Franklin in Frederick Town, Maryland, to discuss the handling of military correspondence through Franklin's postal service. Braddock also put upon Franklin, then the postmaster for the colonies, to assist with the gathering of wagons and supplies. Franklin later wrote in his autobiography that the general expected Fort Duquesne to fall quickly. "Duquesne can hardly detain me above three or four days," boasted the general to Franklin.

Franklin, who had knowledge of Indian ambushes in the colonies and who had participated in negotiations with the natives, cautioned the general against underestimating the enemy. "The only danger I apprehend of obstruction to your march," warned Franklin, "is from ambuscades of Indians, who, by constant practice, are dexterous in laying and executing them, and the slender line, near four miles long, which your army must make, may expose it to be attacked by surprise in its flanks, and to be cut like a thread into several pieces."

"These savages may, indeed, be a formidable enemy to your raw American militia, but upon the King's regular and disciplined troops, sir, it is impossible they should make any impression," scoffed Braddock.

While George Washington had enlisted native assistance the prior year during his failed venture into the Ohio Country, Braddock largely ignored them. Trader and frontiersman George Croghan, then deputy chief to Sir William Johnson, superintendent of northern Indian affairs in New York, met with Braddock and key Indian leaders to attempt an alliance, but Braddock rebuffed them. Many historians have argued that had Braddock enlisted the native allies of the colonies at that point, he would have fared much better.

Eventually, in May, over 2,000 men, including George Washington, began their march, cutting the first road through the wilderness of the Allegheny Mountains. This process, necessary to move wagons and cannon, was slow and arduous. After a while, Braddock split his forces, sending 1,300 soldiers ahead, while the rest, under Colonel Dunbar, continued the work. This "flying column" got ahead of its supply lines, further risking them to the enemy and the elements. Along the way, the soldiers were greeted by rude messages scrawled by the French on trees stripped of their bark.

By July 9, 1755, Braddock's advance force crossed the Monongahela River and was about eight miles from Fort Duquesne. After midday, the British vanguard, in their red coats, was surprised by an enemy force of about 900, about two-thirds natives and one-third French. The war-whoops of the Indians shocked the British soldiers as they attacked from the flanks, catching them in the cross-fire. Meanwhile, in the front, the French blocked their advance. The British responded with muskets and killed the French commander, causing some of the French to flee. However, the natives wisely attacked the British officers first, killing or injuring most of them, and creating a panic among the regulars.

Washington's hat was shot off his head as he tried to rally the men near him, to no avail. He later described them as "as about as much use as trying to halt a stampede of wild bears." By the third hour of battle, the attackers killed or wounded more than half of Braddock's men, and

Braddock's death as the army retreated

sixty of the eighty-six officers were dead or wounded. In confusion, the British soldiers fired upon one another.

Remarkably, George Washington survived several near misses; he later informed his mother that there were four bullet holes in his uniform and that two horses had been shot from underneath him. General Braddock fought bravely, also having several horses shot out from under him before himself being wounded in the arm and abdomen.

In the 19th century, numerous newspapers published a story about Braddock and his fate. These articles recounted a soldier named Thomas Fausett shot Braddock as revenge for how he had treated his brother, another soldier. Both Fausetts were mountain men in the area who fought with the colonials. Thomas witnessed Braddock slashing his brother Joseph with his sword due to Joseph disobeying orders and heading for the cover of the trees. Thomas, also using the trees as cover, pointed his musket at Braddock and shot him in the lungs. Fausett was described by other locals, decades later, as a tough who lived off the wilderness and who was prone to drink.

On April 15, 1951, an article published in the *Roanoke Times* recounted a story passed down through four generations from a colonial soldier, Benjamin Bolling, to his great-grandson William Bolling, then 94 years old. According to family legend, Benjamin Bolling took matters into his own hands during the battle when he acted to protect the lives of his fellow colonials who were being treated like cannon fodder as the British regulars shot through them at the enemy ahead. Bolling turned his musket on Braddock and shot him, believing him to be incompetent. This allowed fellow Virginian George Washington to take command and save the remaining colonials amid the ensuing chaos.

While the integrity of this family tradition and the Fausett legend cannot be proven, others have suggested that his troops may have accidentally shot Braddock. Perhaps it was more than one and not accidental.

Regardless of how he was wounded, Washington and Colonel Nicholas Meriwether lifted Braddock onto a cart. Washington then led what forces he could muster in retreat across the Monongahela. While they left, the natives continued their war whoops and remained behind to scalp the dead and take any remaining prisoners to Fort Duquesne, where they were burned alive.

While on the cart, Braddock ordered Washington to call for Colonel Dunbar to come forward and cover the retreat. Unfortunately, many of Dunbar's men, upon hearing of the vicious attack, had already fled.

As the army retreated, Braddock died four days later, on July 13, at Great Meadows. The chaplain wounded, Washington personally officiated the burial ceremony and retained Braddock's sash for the remainder of his life, wearing it throughout the American Revolution and his presidency. Braddock was buried beneath the road and covered by retreating wagon tracks so the enemy would not find his body.

Washington took on Braddock's servant, Thomas Bishop. This man served Washington as his valet at Mount Vernon into the 1790s. The French continued to hold the Ohio Valley for three more years.

In 1804, what were believed to be Braddock's remains were discovered buried in the roadway close to Great Meadows. Some of the bones were taken as souvenirs. A local magistrate got word of the desecration of the grave and asked for the bones to be returned. These bones and others found at the site were reburied on a hilltop by a prominent tree. A sign was hung on the tree to mark the spot. Other souvenirs were later shipped to the Peale Museum in Philadelphia which was purchased by P.T. Barnum. He moved the contents of the museum to his American Museum in New York City, but it burned to the ground in 1865. A section of vertebrae is reportedly in the collection of the Walter Reed Museum in Bethesda, Maryland. In 1913, a monument was erected by the Coldstream Guards in his honor near the site of the tree.

To this day, sections of this road are known as Braddock's Road, following closely US Route 40 in Pennsylvania and Maryland. Braddock is also the namesake of the towns of Braddock, Mount Braddock, Braddock Hills, and North Braddock in Pennsylvania; Braddock Heights or Braddock Mountain near Frederick, Maryland; and Braddock Middle School in Cumberland, Maryland.

Besides US Route 40, there are Braddock Roads in Cumberland, Maryland, between Alexandria and Aldie, Virginia, and in Alexandria

The original resting place of General Edward Braddock

proper. The Metrorail station at that location is so named. There is also a Braddock Street in Winchester, Virginia.

Fort Necessity National Battlefield, along US Route 40, is run by the National Park Service. Visitors can see the initial burial site of General Braddock on a section of the original Braddock Road, northwest of Fort Necessity. His current burial site under the monument is a few hundred yards away, near a parking lot. Across the way is the Braddock

The General Braddock Monument

Inn Restaurant, which serves country fare and drinks. There you can have a pint and imagine the army marching past the door on its ill-fated expedition.

The site where Braddock was shot is now known as Braddock's Field in Braddock, Pennsylvania, near the junction of Turtle Creek and the

Monongahela River. There are historic markers there and a historical society in North Braddock. This was also the site where Washington went to warn the French in 1754.

If you are interested in seeing Fort Duquesne, which Braddock never reached, it is in downtown Pittsburgh at Point State Park. There you will find the blockhouse from Fort Pitt, the Fort Pitt Museum and an outline of the former Fort Duquesne. The museum, run by the Commonwealth of Pennsylvania, includes exhibits about the French and Indian War and the American Revolution.

4.

GIA MARIE CARANGI

"Pennsylvania's Supermodel"

County: Bucks • Town: Feasterville
Buried at Sunset Memorial Park
333 County Line Road

This young woman went from working in her father's Philadelphia luncheonette to becoming what many consider to be the world's first supermodel. As a child, she went through a turbulent home life when her parents divorced. As a young adult, she learned about life in the fast lane first at Philadelphia clubs and later partying at Studio 54. She became active in the drug world and wound up a heroin addict. She went to the top of the fashion world only to fall into a life that included theft, prostitution, and violence. She was one of the first women in the United States to pass away as a result of AIDS. Her life was a true roller coaster, and her name was Gia Marie Carangi though her fame in the modeling world resulted in her simply being known as Gia.

Gia was born in Philadelphia on January 29, 1960. Her father, Joseph Carangi, was a restaurateur who operated a chain of shops called Hoagie City. Her mother, Kathleen Adams Carangi, was a homemaker who was eleven years younger than her husband when she walked down the aisle at the age of twenty-one. The couple produced three children in three years, two sons and then the daughter they named Gia. Joseph also had a daughter from a previous failed marriage. The relationship between Joe Carangi and his wife was a rocky one. He left home early so he could catch the breakfast crowd and generally didn't return until after his employees had finished cleaning up his shops for the day. This was

Gia Carangi

often late at night, and so the time he was able to spend with his children was limited. Even as he grew more successful, which enabled his wife to purchase expensive clothes, including furs, her complaints and dissatisfaction with their lives seemed to grow. Their arguments grew physical. According to Gia's mother, it reached the point where she believed that "he was going to kill me or I was going to kill him." In February of 1972, Kathleen Carangi left her husband and her children. The separation and ultimate divorce had a profound effect on the eleven-year-old Gia.

Gia never felt truly loved by either of her parents. She viewed her father as favoring her brothers, and her mother's affection became something she seemed to pursue throughout her short life. Many who knew her would point to her parent's breakup and the emotional trauma it brought their daughter for her failure to function successfully as an adult. Some also view the episode as being a prime factor in the drug dependency that would come to haunt her. Entering her adolescent years, Gia sought out the attention of other teenage girls, often sending them flowers. Some viewed this as an attempt to receive the motherly love she felt had been denied. While that may have played a role, Gia was physically attracted to other girls, and that would be the case throughout her short life.

She attended Abraham Lincoln High School, located in northeast Philadelphia. It was while attending Lincoln that she became one of "the Bowie kids." These were kids who were obsessed with the rock star David Bowie and tried to emulate, as best they could, his public persona and lifestyle. Gia was attracted by Bowie's fashion sense and his outspoken bisexuality.

By this time, Gia's mother had remarried and her stepfather, Henry Sperr, was convinced that Bowie or perhaps music, in general, had changed her. As told by Gia's biographer, Stephen Fried, in his book *Thing Of Beauty,* Sperr recounted that "She got a Bowie haircut and that changed her personality completely. She seemed like a sweet, young kid before, and then afterward . . . well, you know it probably had something to do with the drugs. She would be disrespectful; she would constantly be fighting, just over nothing." The reference to drugs came from the fact that at the time, drugs were readily available at Lincoln High. As a matter of fact, according to Fried, "phenobarbs were everywhere . . . Students were throwing them across the 107 Lunchroom like confetti, swallowing them like candy."

Gia's modeling career began in Philadelphia. At the suggestion of a friend, Gia's mother sent her to be photographed by Joe Petrellis, a well-known commercial photographer based in center-city Philadelphia. Gia was fourteen at the time, and the session with Petrellis failed to produce anything close to the glamour shots for which she would become noted. It was worthwhile in that it created an interest in the young girl's mind. She enjoyed being the center of attention and wanted to learn more about the art of photography. By the time she was seventeen, her modeling career had blossomed to the point where she was being featured in Philadelphia newspaper ads.

One person who was very influential in Gia's rise in Philadelphia was Maurice Tannenbaum, a Philadelphia hairstylist who was known as Mr. Maurice. He had reached a point where he thought he had gone as far as he could in the styling business and wanted to try something new. The new thing turned out to be photography. Mr. Maurice first noticed Gia on the dance floor of a Philadelphia club. He approached her and asked if she'd be willing to do some test shots with him. The first session went so well that they made it a weekly habit, and they began to get together every Thursday night. In recalling those sessions, Mr. Maurice said, "She just let the camera have it. She didn't hold back. If the camera didn't like her, it was the cameras fault." Mr. Maurice also used the meetings to get to know Gia. As he recalled, she had already done almost everything by the time she was sixteen. "She had tried almost every drug, had all kinds of sex, and was going with a very fast crowd." He also noticed that she enjoyed being the center of attention.

In the long run, it may have been Mr. Maurice, who set in motion the events that would make Gia a supermodel. He hired a former model as a makeup artist. This model had remained on good terms with her former agent Wilhelmina Behmenburg Cooper who ran Wilhelmina Models Inc. out of New York City. The makeup artist offered to show Maurice's portfolio, which largely consisted of photos of Gia, to Wilhelmina. This showing resulted in invites to both Gia and Maurice to visit New York, at their own expense, for a meeting.

Most of the young women who showed up at the modeling agency were put through a screening process. This wasn't the case with Gia as both her and Maurice were quickly taken in to meet Wilhelmina. According to Maurice, Wilhelmina was awed by the young girl who had entered her office. She spoke in glowing terms about Gia's future as a model. She left the agency with a contract in hand and instructions to talk to her parents. At the age of seventeen, Gia had wowed the head of one of the most influential modeling agencies in New York.

Wilhelmina had her own successful career as a model and also exerted a steadying effect on Gia. Under Wilhelmina's wing, she worked at making it as a model. Keeping appointments and attending various classes taught by the agency. The awe that Wilhelmina felt for Gia was reciprocal, and for a time, Gia did as she was instructed. On one visit to one of her uncles, Gia told him that she had found a mother.

In October of 1978, Gia reported to a session with Chris von Wangenheim, a famous fashion photographer. The session produced a page in *Vogue.* During the shoot, she also posed nude behind a chain-link fence. For some of the later shots, Gia was joined by makeup artist Sandy Linter. The meeting with Sandy resulted in an infatuation on Gia's part and an on and off relationship that would last her whole life.

After just one year in New York, Gia had become a sought after established model. *Vogue* described her rise as "meteoric." The famous portrait photographer Francesco Scavullo wrote that "Everyone was nuts about her" in his 1982 book titled *Scavullo Women.* He also described Gia in this work as "old, young, decadent, innocent, volatile, vulnerable, and more tough-spirited than she looks." Scavullo was hardly the only photographer drawn to Gia. She also worked with Arthur Elgort, Denis Piel, and Richard Avalon. She graced the covers of multiple magazines, including *Cosmopolitan* and *Vogue.* She also was a major force in multiple advertising campaigns for established fashion houses, including Armani and Christian Dior.

As one of, if not the leading model in New York at the time, it is no surprise that she became a regular at Studio 54. Like many of the patrons, she began using cocaine on her visits to the club. John Long was a friend of Gia's who accompanied her to the Studio several times. As he recalled in *Thing of Beauty,* "We liked to dance together, and she used me to meet girls. It's not easy for a girl to score with other girls. She could get any man she wanted but said she envied me because I had a better chance of scoring with Juli Foster than she did. Juli Foster was a big Wilhelmina model at the time, and Gia had a crush on her. Gia would say, 'Ask that girl to dance.' Then she'd join with us and pull the girl into a corner and buy her a beer."

Maurice Tannenbaum also recalls Gia as a woman struggling to cope with her sexual identity. "She was a lesbian who grew up at a time when that was unacceptable. I would see her trying to be a woman at Studio 54. She wasn't. That's not what Gia was. One night she was there in this red dress . . . She was trying to be this feminine model, you know, a New York celebrity, and it just didn't fit. She was more comfortable in a jeans jacket and jeans and country boots with a T-shirt. The world expected one thing of her, and she was something else."

It was while partying at another club, the CBGB, that she became a fan of the musical group Blondie. It was not unusual for visitors to Gia's New York apartment to find her listening to the band's music. When *Philadelphia* magazine included her in their hot people to watch edition in 1979, she invited the magazine editor into her apartment, where she never turned down her stereo that was playing the band's newest release. Gia also appeared in a Blondie video for the song "Atomic."

Though she had already been living in the fast lane, Gia's destructive tendencies increased after her mentor and substitute mother, Wilhelmina Cooper, passed away in March of 1980 from lung cancer. The young model was devastated by the loss and began to seriously abuse drugs, including heroin, to which she developed an addiction.

It was at this point that Gia began her career decline. Her drug use took its effect on both her work, her personality, and of course, her finances. She began to miss photo sessions, throw temper tantrums, and leave scheduled work assignments to score drugs to support her habit. In *Thing of Beauty* Fried includes a photo of a page from Gia's datebook that includes a reminder she had scribbled to herself to get heroin.

Late in 1980, Gia left Wilhelmina Models and signed with the Ford Model Agency. Ford had been founded in 1946 and had earned a reputation as an elite and innovative agency. Her relationship with Ford was short-lived. In one of her last sessions for *Vogue,* she was positioned in a wooden chair in a spaghetti-strap dress. In one instance, she fell asleep in the chair and in another injected herself with heroin during the session, which resulted in blood flowing down her arm. It was too much for the magazine which decided to cease doing business with her. Ford dropped her after only a few weeks.

In addition to her career, her personal life was in disarray as well. Old friends didn't want any association with her, fearing it could harm their own opportunities. Sandy Linter, with whom Gia had an on and off relationship, stopped taking her phone calls. In February of 1981, Gia decided to move back to Philadelphia and attempt to kick her drug habit.

Attempting to get sober, Gia went through a 21-day detox program. Her recovery was short-lived. On March 22, one of suburban Philadelphia's finest was in the area of an apartment complex where had been assigned to do surveillance. He watched a red sports car speeding down the street where it collided with a fence at the end of a dead-end. The car then backed up and drove quickly away. The driver then led the officer on a highspeed chase that ended only after other officers had been alerted and blocked off an intersection. Gia was the driver and was immediately taken into custody, where she was found to be under the influence of alcohol and cocaine.

Still struggling with addiction, Gia attempted to make a comeback as a model. Her last appearance on an American magazine cover was in April of 1982 when *Cosmopolitan* featured her. By the end of that year, those who were willing to work with her were few and far between. She was sent home from Tunisia for using heroin during her final photoshoot for a German mail-order clothing company. In 1983 she left New York for good. By this point in her life, the money she had made as a supermodel had been squandered on drugs, and she was stealing from friends to support her habit.

In the final years of her life, she would alternately get clean and then slip back into using drugs. She spent six months in 1985, getting clean as a patient at Eagleville Hospital in Norristown. After leaving the hospital, she stayed clean for a few months before feeding her addiction again. She was living in Atlantic City at least part of the time where she supported her drug habit through prostitution. By late in the year, Gia was convinced she had AIDS. Deeply depressed, she attempted to kill herself by

Gia Carangi's grave

overdosing on heroin. In June of 1986, she was admitted to Warminster Hospital, where she was officially diagnosed to be suffering from AIDS. Four months later, she was admitted to Hahnemann Hospital. In the view of her biographer, it was during her hospital stay that she resolved her relationship with her mother. He reported that one of Gia's counselors told him that, "My perception of what happened, in the end, was that Gia wanted this type of nurturing from her mom, and she set it up so that she got it before she died." Gia passed away on November 18, 1986. She was 26 years old. She was laid to rest in Sunset Memorial Park, located in Feasterville, Pennsylvania.

In 1998 Angelina Jolie starred as Gia in a biographical film made by HBO. The film was generally well-received by critics. Jolie won both a Golden Globe and a Screen Actors Guild award for her performance.

As detailed in *Thing of Beauty* and mentioned previously, Gia was a big fan of the rock group Blondie. In that work, Fried quotes the group's song "Die Young Stay Pretty," which contains the lyric "Deteriorate in your own time, leave only the best behind, you gotta live fast cause it won't last." It could have been a eulogy.

5.

LINDA DARNELL

"Hollywood Beauty"

County: Chester County • Town: Kennett Square
Buried at Union Hill Cemetery
424 North Union Street

Linda Darnell's life reads like a movie script in which she could have starred. Unfortunately, the movie would be a tragedy instead of a triumph. She left home at fifteen, driven by her mother to become rich and famous, to live the Hollywood dream. She appeared in forty-six films and won international acclaim but was unable to cope with the pressures of Hollywood and was caught in a downward spiral of alcoholism, failed marriages, and exploitive relationships. She died tragically at forty-one.

Darnell was born Monetta Eloyse Darnell in Dallas, Texas, on October 16, 1923. She was one of four children to Calvin Roy Darnell and Margaret "Pearl" Brown. Her dad called her Tweedles the night she was born, and she would always remain Tweedles to her family.

She was a beautiful child, and her mother encouraged her to model. By the age of eleven, she was modeling clothes for an area department store. She had no trouble getting modeling jobs because her beauty was so striking that most clients and agencies thought she was five or six years older than she was.

When Darnell was in the sixth grade, Pearl learned there was to be a talent contest at a local school. She made Darnell enter. She won first place for singing "Alice Blue Gown." From then on, Darnell didn't have much time for anything else. Pearl was determined they'd go to Hollywood.

Linda Darnell

The following quote from Darnell years later says it all: "Mother really shoved me along, spotting me in one contest after another. I had no great talent, and I didn't want to be a movie star particularly. But mother had always wanted it for herself, and I guess she attained it through me.

By the time Darnell was thirteen, she was acting in local theater companies, including the Dallas Little Theater, where she was cast in the Southwestern premiere of *Murder in the Cathedral*. That same year (1936), she was hired as one of the hostesses at the Texas Centennial Exposition. In November 1937, a talent scout for 20th Century Fox came to Dallas looking for new faces. Pushed by her mother, Darnell met him, and he was impressed by her beauty and poise and invited her for a screen test in Hollywood. In February 1938, she and Pearl made the trek to California, but when her real age became known, she was sent home.

Two years later and after more local theater appearances, Darnell was signed to a contract with 20th Century Fox. Darnell flew to Los Angeles alone on April 5, 1939, and went on salary the next day at $75 a week.

Darryl Zanuck was the vice-president in charge of production at the time and was convinced that Darnell had the looks to grow into a saleable commodity. It was Zanuck who decided to change her name to Darnell feeling that it would better advertise her beauty and suggest a Latin quality that matched her coloring. He immediately cast her in *Hotel for Women*. The role came to her when Loretta Young, assigned initially to play the role, demanded a salary which the studio would not pay. Darnell was only fifteen at the time, but she was passing as seventeen and being listed as nineteen. Shooting began in April and was completed in June. Although exciting, Darnell admitted that making movies was not what she'd expected it would be. She hadn't realized the amount of work that went into it.

Zanuck was thrilled with Darnell's work in *Hotel for Women* and promised to find something else for her right away. She was cast alongside Henry Fonda and Claudette Colbert in *Drums Along the Mohawk*, replacing Dorris Bowdon in a sudden and insensitive way. Later Zanuck changed his mind feeling the role was too small for Darnell and returned Bowdon to the role. Darnell was quickly cast opposite Tyrone Power in the light romantic comedy *Day-Time Wife*. She received excellent reviews and was quickly cast in the drama-comedy *Star Dust*. The film received good reviews and boosted Darnell's popularity, and her salary went to $200 a week.

Her first big-budget film was *Brigham Young* in 1940 opposite Tyrone Power again. They became a highly publicized onscreen couple, and Zanuck took advantage of it by adding romantic scenes. The movie made her a star, and that summer, she was again working with Power in a big-budget adventure film, *The Mark of Zorro*. The critics raved, and it was a box office sensation. She was next paired with Henry Fonda in the

Linda Darnell in a May 1944 pin-up photo for Yank, *the Army weekly*

western *Chad Hanna*, which got little attention, but Darnell returned to the critics' good graces when again working with Tyrone Power in *Blood and Sand*.

Darnell's career took a dip after *Blood and Sand*, as the studio claimed to be unable to find suitable roles. Months went by without any work, and she realized that Darryl Zanuck had lost interest in her.

During her first stay in Hollywood, her relationship with her mother worsened. Her mother was an unpopular figure on the lot due to her overbearing and possessive behavior. As a publicity woman put it, "Darnell's success went to her mother's head."

Dorris Bowdon remembered, "she must have offended, irritated, or annoyed everybody she came in contact with. The record shows that every film Darnell worked on, the people in charge had trouble with the mother."

Finally, Pearl was barred from the lot, forbidden to enter the studio gates. Following an intense fight between her parents in 1942, Darnell left home with her younger sister, Monte, and never returned. Also, in 1942, she was plagued with extortion letters threatening bodily harm unless $2,000 was paid. Eventually, a seventeen-year-old high school student was arrested for the crime.

In the early 1940s, she was cast in roles she hated and in films that didn't do well. She was passed over for parts she wanted and could have easily done. On April 18, 1943, at age 19, Darnell eloped with a 42-year-old cameraman, Peverell Marley, in Las Vegas. Marley was a heavy drinker and introduced Darnell to alcohol, which led to many other problems such as addiction and weight gain.

Most friends and relatives disapproved of the marriage, including 20th Century Fox and Darryl Zanuck, who was so upset he suspended her from making films.

In 1944 she was named one of the four most beautiful women in Hollywood, along with Hedy Lamarr, Ingrid Bergman, and Gene Tierney in an edition of *Look* magazine. This led to the studio allowing her to be loaned out for the lead in *Summer Storm*. This film provided her with a new screen image as a pin-up girl. Her boost in popularity gave her the confidence to pursue a role she badly wanted, and she prodded Zanuck into casting her in *Hangover Square*. The film was such a success that it brought Darnell back to prominence and led to her being added to the cast of *Fallen Angel*, which included Dana Andrews and Alice Faye.

Darnell was terrified by director Otto Preminger who she grew to despise, but her performance was praised by reviewers so widely that there was talk of an Oscar nomination.

In 1946 during the production of *Centennial Summer*, Darnell repeatedly met with Howard Hughes. Although she initially disregarded gossip of an affair, she fell in love with the womanizing millionaire and separated from Pev Marley and filed for divorce. She was madly in love with Hughes and dating him around the same time as Ava Gardner. When Hughes's plane crashed and critically injured him, she was one of the first to visit him. Shortly afterward, Hughes broke her heart by announcing that he had no desire to marry her and ended the relationship. Darnell returned to her husband and canceled divorce proceedings.

She received some of the best reviews of her career when *My Darling Clementine* was released in 1946. She co-starred with Henry Fonda and Victor Mature. Shortly after, she won the starring role in the highly anticipated *Forever Amber*, based on a bestselling historical novel. She was happily surprised to get the job despite having to work with Otto Preminger. She was sure that *Forever Amber* would be her ticket to stardom. The movie did not live up to its hype. It was a box office success, but a critical disappointment and it did not gain her the recognition for which she had hoped. Later, whenever she mentioned the picture to friends, she referred to it as Forever Under.

In 1948, Darnell and Marley adopted a daughter, Charlotte Mildred "Lola" Marley, the actress's only child. But, by mid-1948, Darnell became romantically involved with her director, Joseph Mankiewicz, while working on *A Letter to Three Wives*. She filed again for divorce. The affair went on for six years, but Mankiewicz was unwilling to leave his wife. Darnell again returned to her husband. While the romance was a failure, the movie was a huge success and recorded her most famous line. Her classic line came in response to an older friend's suggestion, "If I was you, I'd show more of what I got. Maybe wear somethin' with beads." Darnell replied, "What I got don't need beads."

Darnell had been widely expected to be nominated for an Academy Award for *A Letter to Three Wives*, and when that didn't happen, her career began to wane. Aside from *No Way Out* in 1950, her later films were rarely noteworthy, and her appearances sporadic. (*No Way Out* was directed by Joseph Mankiewicz and was a groundbreaking movie about racial tension and included Sidney Poitier in his screen debut.) Her alcoholism and weight gain further complicated the situation. She became very depressed when she discovered she didn't get a part she wanted so badly in the film *The Barefoot Contessa*, which was written, produced, and directed by Mankiewicz. She learned from trade papers that Ava Gardner had been cast in the part. It was a humiliation from which she would never recover.

Darnell was granted a divorce from Marley in 1951 and was granted custody of Lola. In 1954 she married Philip Liebmann, a brewery heir, but that shortly ended in another divorce. She would try marriage once more with Merle Robertson, a pilot, in 1957. In 1963 they divorced after bouts of heavy drinking, deep depression, and stints in rehab.

With the studios cutting back on production, film offers were few and far between. The competition of television forced studios all over Hollywood to drop actors. Darnell had long intended to attempt the stage, and now it became essential. She planned to test her skills far enough from either coast that none of the major critics would review her. She decided to make her debut at the Sombrero Playhouse in Phoenix, Arizona, in *A Roomful of Roses*. She spent six weeks studying for her part and rehearsing lines. In mid-February 1956, when she arrived in Phoenix, the word had gotten out, and critics had come flocking into town. Her reviews were good as it turned out, and she signed on to do *Tea and Sympathy* at the Coconut Grove Playhouse in Miami. She later went on tour with the show all over the country, and at one point, the cast included Burt Reynolds.

Her travels were interrupted enough for her to do television shows like *The Twentieth Century Fox Hour*, *Playhouse 90*, and *The Ford Television Theatre* and appear in episodes of *Wagon Train* and *77 Sunset Strip*. She made a final film appearance in the B-western *Black Spurs* in 1965.

Linda Darnell died on April 10, 1965, from burns she received in a house fire in Glenview, Illinois, the day before. She was transferred to

Linda Darnell's grave

the burn unit at Chicago's Cook County Hospital with burns over 80 percent of her body. She lingered for an agonizing thirty-three hours. The fire was caused by careless smoking.

Darnell's body was cremated. She had requested her ashes be scattered over a ranch in New Mexico. Because of a dispute with the landowners, that was not done. After the remains had been in storage in a Chicago funeral home for ten years, her daughter requested that they be interred at the Union Hill Cemetery in Chester County, Pennsylvania, in the family plot of her son-in-law.

For her contribution to the motion picture industry, Linda Darnell has a star on the Hollywood Walk of Fame. She died at 41 and in a tragic manner. "You know, I never felt accepted in the movie world," she confessed near the end, "I think that's why I resent my family so. I would never have been an actress if it hadn't been for mother's insisting. To think I paid a psychiatrist $25,000 trying to work through all that before he gave up on me."

6.

DARR MINE DISASTER

"Into the Abyss"

County: Westmoreland • Town: Smithton
Buried at Olive Branch Cemetery
Route 981 and Van Meter Road

The Darr Mine disaster is just another chapter in America's sad history of coal mining disasters. Since 1870, 51,504 boys and men have been killed in mining accidents. The Darr disaster claimed 239 lives in December 1907 and is the worst mining disaster in Pennsylvania history. That month would prove to be the deadliest in United States mining history. Over 704 miners lost their lives in five explosions in four different states. Just days before the Darr explosion, on December 6, the Monongah Mine in West Virginia exploded, and 362 miners were killed. It is considered the worst mining disaster in U.S. history.

On December 19, 1907, at approximately 11:30 A.M., a blast ripped through underground tunnels and rooms, bending iron railroad rails, demolishing wooden coal cars, and embedding coal dust in the ends of collapsed wooden pillars that had supported the roof. People in the vicinity of the mine describe the explosion as an awful rumbling, followed by a loud report and a concussion that shook the nearby buildings and was felt within a radius of several miles. At the same time, there came out of the mouth of the mine, an immense cloud of smoke and dust that floated across the Youghiogheny River. The concussion broke windows in Jacob's Creek on the far bank and struck like a dagger in the hearts of those still at home, for there was no doubt what the sound and vibration meant. The explosion had been so terrific in its force that the inspectors were

The unidentified dead from the Darr mine disaster

convinced upon a superficial investigation that it would be impossible for any of the entombed workers to be rescued alive.

There are conflicting accounts as to whether one or two men survived. For sure, Joseph Mapleton survived. He was what was known as a pumper and left his work site to get some oil. He recalled, "I was near Entry Number 21 when I heard an awful rumbling. I started toward the entry, but the next instant, I was blinded, and for a little time, I did not know anything. Then I got to the side entry and worked my way out." After having some wounds quickly dressed, he would join the rescue parties being organized by the mine superintendent. According to other sources, a miner by the name of Thomas A. Williams also survived after his coal car was blown fifty feet, the coal car likely saving his life.

The rescuers found that the roof had collapsed 1500 feet in from the mouth, which blocked any quick access to the men. One of the first bodies found was that of mine foreman, William Campbell, who had been decapitated. His wife told of his fears of gas and a lack of ventilation in the months preceding the explosion. He had informed the company of his concerns, and a new ventilation shaft was in the process of being sunk. It is quite possible that the disaster would have been avoided if the men had one more day to dig forty feet to reach the new shaft.

Over a week later, by December 27, only 124 bodies had been recovered. Workers turned up bodies until February 22, 1908. The grief was palpable, and more than some could bear. One man "went insane" and committed suicide, while a wife and mother who lost her husband and two sons tried to drown herself in the river.

The explosion had left 239 men and boys dead, 130 widows, 300 children without fathers, and 542 people without a source of income. Men and boys from Italy, Hungary, Austria, Germany, Poland, and the United States were among those who perished.

Despite the considerable loss of life in the Darr Mine disaster, the death toll could have been much worse had it not been for what is referred to as the Miracle of St. Nicholas. Many of the miners were of the Greek Orthodox faith, and December 19 is a religious holiday, the Feast of St. Nicholas. Usually, there would be about 400 miners working at the mine, but between 200 and 250 miners chose to celebrate the holiday and forfeit a day's pay. Instead of being in the mine, they were at church in Jacob's Creek when they felt the blast shake the building.

Nineteen miners were never found; it was presumed that their bodies were buried under roof falls and debris. The remainder of those who were capable of recognition ranged in age from 14 to 56. Boys in coal mining families often went to work in the mines, many of them to work alongside their fathers. Many parents with large families relied on their boys for income and often lied about their sons' ages to get jobs. Mine companies also evaded the law by not listing boys on their payroll and paying the boys wages to their fathers.

The company, the Pittsburgh Coal Company (now CONSOL Energy), paid for the funerals of all the victims. They also paid $300 to widows or parents for each of those lost.

The search for the cause of the explosion would lead to three reports: one from the company's experts, another from the coroner's jury, and a third from the Pennsylvania Department of Mines. All reached different conclusions. Workers who went into off-limits areas, miners who had open flames for illumination, lack of timely mine inspections, poor ventilation of mine gas and coal dust, and an accidental explosion of dynamite were all cited as possible causes. Only the state Department of Mines found any fault with the management of the mine. The report read, "We are of the opinion that had well-known safeguards, such as ample and sufficient ventilation, the use of safety explosives, the thorough wetting and laying of dust, the use of locked safety lamps, the employment of shot firers, and the maintenance of rigid discipline been employed in the Darr Mine, this calamity would not have occurred." Even this report failed to mention what the miners had been saying for quite some time before the explosion—the mine was very gaseous and dangerous.

Monument at the mass grave of Darr mine disaster victims

The victims were buried in various cemeteries in Westmoreland and surrounding counties. A stone memorial recalls the miners and their fate in the Olive Branch Cemetery in Belle Vernon, erected in 1909 by the Hungarian-American Federation. The Pennsylvania Historical and Museum Commission erected a historic site marker on Route 981, which runs past the cemetery. The large stone memorial marks the graves of seventy-one victims of the explosion, including forty-nine who were not identified. The Belle Vernon Rotary Club erected another stone memorial that reads: "Darr Mine Disaster. On December 19, 1907, just south of Van Meter, Pennsylvania, an explosion ripped through the Darr mine, killing 239 miners. One of the worst disasters in the nation. This prompted the ban of open flame mine lamps.

7.

20+ DONORA SMOG VICTIMS

"Clean Air Started Here"

County: Washington • Town: Monongahela
Most are buried at Monongahela Cemetery
800 Country Club Road

Smoky air was a sign of progress in the small Pennsylvania city of Donora in Washington County, less than 25 miles south-southeast of Pittsburgh, wrapped by a semicircular bend in the Monongahela River. Pollution from two of the major employers, the American Steel and Wire plant and the Donora Zinc Works, was a sign of economic activity and an accepted part of life. These firms employed more than half of all workers in Donora. In October 1948, many citizens remembered the days of the Great Depression when the air was cleaner due to an unwelcome reduction in production and an increase in layoffs. The country had boomed during World War II, but an economic downturn followed the peace at the same time Winston Churchill ominously spoke of an Iron Curtain descending across Europe. The USA was, fortunately, experiencing a modest upturn in 1948, and people were focused on their families, their work, and the presidential campaign between Republican Thomas E. Dewey and the incumbent Harry S. Truman.

During the last week of October, few in Donora paid attention as the smog from the plants began to build up, though many began coughing. What made this smog more pungent than usual was a severe temperature inversion affecting the region. Warm air above a layer of cold air near the ground was trapping the pollution, leaving it nowhere to go. Besides, the town was situated on a bend in the river, further concentrating the smog. Floating in the mass of filthy yellowish air were hydrogen fluoride,

The Donora smog

fluorine, nitrogen dioxide, sulfur dioxide, sulfuric acid, and other poisonous emissions from the plants.

On Friday, October 29th, the annual Halloween parade continued as scheduled. Children displayed their colorful costumes as they marched down an unusually smoky Main Street. Later, Chief John Volk and Russell Davis of the fire department began responding to calls for help. They set up oxygen tents for those in need but quickly ran out of the gas.

Doctors, in this town of 14,000, began making urgent house calls, often seeing patients who were usually treated by others. People were reporting family members who were struggling to breathe. They were panicking and calling every doctor in town, trying to find help as the smog got worse—so bad that driving was nearly impossible. Said fireman Davis, "I drove on the left side of the street with my head out the window. Steering by scraping the curb." Many people gave up driving to the hospital because they could not see. As the hospitals became overwhelmed, ambulances began taking victims to Pittsburgh. One victim died on the way. Another was later found dead on the street.

The following day, Saturday, October 30th, at the residence of Milton Elmer Hall of Webster, a World War I veteran and employee of the Zinc Works, his seventeen-year-old son, Charles, started to cough and sneeze. The veteran who himself had been suffering the last twelve years from illness suggested the lad take some aspirin. Charles's mother had passed away when he was ten, leaving him and his four older siblings motherless. Also, that afternoon, the local Donora Dragons High School hosted their homecoming football game. No passes were thrown due to poor visibility. Fans sitting in the stands could not see the field.

By mid-day, Saturday, Cora Vernon of the American Red Cross arranged for all calls to doctors' offices to be switched to an emergency center established at the town hall. Telephone calls for help had been delayed for up to six hours due to the high volume overwhelming the operators.

Later that day, rain began to fall and gradually reduce the smog. Also, later that day, Elmer Hall breathed in too much smog. He turned to his son, Charles, and collapsed dead in his arms.

Downtown, the fire chief and his assistant began borrowing oxygen from neighboring McKeesport, Monessen, and Charleroi. Said Volk, "I didn't take any myself. What I did every time I came back to the station was have a little shot of whiskey."

Finally, on Sunday at 6 A.M., the leadership of the plants held a meeting and agreed to shut down. They did so until the rain cleared the air of the smog.

As the fog lifted that Sunday, twenty citizens of Donora had died—most of them elderly or with respiratory problems. Fifty more had been hospitalized, and hundreds more had been treated. Thousands had experienced symptoms that went untreated.

Said Dr. William Rongaus of the local board of health, "It's murder. There's nothing else you can call it. There's something in the air here that isn't found elsewhere. There was smog in Monessen, too, but it didn't kill people there." Dr. Rongaus further stated that though those that died were mostly elderly, he treated many young, healthy people that were having trouble breathing. "I treated many victims who never had any symptoms of asthma. All complained of severe pains in the lower chest. It seemed to me like some sort of partial paralysis of the diaphragm."

Norbert Hockman, a local chemist, surmised the culprit was sulfur trioxide, which formed when sulfur dioxide mixes with the air. It is poisonous when inhaled. This gas was most likely the output of the zinc operation. Another expert pointed out that most of the victims lived within eight blocks of the zinc plant.

Those who died were mostly older and suffered from heart or lung ailments. Many were recent immigrants who had worked at the plants. They included:

Donora Smog Victim	Age	Residence	Cemetery	Town
Ivan Ceh	69	464 rear 5th Ave, Donora	Saint Dominic	Donora
Barbara Chinchar	55	50 Watkins Ave, Donora	Saint Michaels	Donora
Taylor Circle	81	725 Heslep Ave, Donora	Monongahela	Monongahela
John Cunningham	63	322 10th St., Donora	Monongahela	Monongahela
Bernardo DiSanza	67	337 3rd St., Donora	Saint Dominic	Donora
Michael Dorincz	84	539 Ohio St., Donora		
William Gardiner	66	440 McKean Ave Donora	Monongahela	Monongahela
Suzanna Gnora	62	Donora Plan Box 883	Saint Michaels	Donora
Milton Elmer Hall	52	Webster Hollow	Fells Church	Fellsburg
Emma Hobbs	55	Webster	Monongahela	Monongahela
Ignace Hollowiti	64	83 Allen Plan, Donora		
Jeanie Kirkwood	67	121 Ida Ave, Donora	Monongahela	Monongahela
Marcel Kraska	65	715 4th St., Donora		
Andrew Odelga	69	450 8th St., Donora		
Ida Orr	58	Fellsburg	Monongahela	Monongahela
Thomas Amos Short	81	Webster	Monongahela	Monongahela
Peter Paul Stankovich	67	Wilco Hill below Webster		
Perry Stevens	55	88 Bank St., Donora		
Sawka Trubolis	65	438 6th St., Donora		
John West	51	River Rd., Sunnyside	Monoogahela	Monongahela

Within a month of the incident, fifty more individuals died, including Lukasz Musial, the father of Hall of Fame baseball player and 1948 National League Most Valuable Player, Stan Musial.

Researchers reviewing the autopsy results found lethal fluorine levels more than twenty times normal. Fluorine gas was a byproduct of the zinc smelting process. The focus turned to the Zinc Works. Curiously, no vegetation lived within a half-mile of the plant. Another researcher calculated thousands of more residents could have died if the smog had lasted longer.

Smog victim Jeanie Kirkwood

During the ensuing years, lawsuits against the parent company, U.S. Steel, followed, but the company never accepted responsibility stating the accident was "an act of God." Eventually, in 1951, they settled with over 80 victims out of court, paying out $235,000. This left considerably less than $3000 each after legal expenses. American Steel and Wire settled for more than $4.6 million due to 130 claimants. This was only 5% of the damages sought. The company was prepared to show that the

Grave of smog victim Milton Emler Hall

49

smog was caused by "freak weather conditions" and that the smoke came from many sources other than the factory, including railroads, homes, and automobiles. U.S. Steel ultimately closed both plants by 1966.

On a positive note, the story of the Donora Smog was often cited, in addition to Rachel Carson's book *Silent Spring*, as helping the clean-air movement, which resulted in the Clean Air Act of 1963.

A historical marker was placed downtown at the 50th anniversary in 1998. The Donora Smog Museum, which records the history of the incident, opened in 2008. Unfortunately for Donora, the population of the town is now only one-third of its peak.

Hillside with unmarked graves of poor victims of the Donora smog

8.

DANIEL DRAWBAUGH

"The Edison of the Cumberland Valley"

County: Cumberland • Town: Shiremanstown
Buried at Saint John's Cemetery
4605 East Trindle Road

The history books say Alexander Graham Bell invented the telephone in 1876. But the reality was not that cut and dried. Numerous people were tinkering and experimenting with transmitting voice electronically over telegraph wires during the mid to late 1800s besides Bell, including Daniel Drawbaugh, Amos Dolbear, Thomas Edison, Elisha Gray, Antonio Meucci, and Philip Reis. It was Daniel Drawbaugh of Eberly's Mills, Pennsylvania, who came within one vote by a U.S. Supreme Court justice of being declared the inventor of the telephone.

Daniel Drawbaugh was born July 14, 1827, in Allen (now Lower Allen) Township, Cumberland County, Pennsylvania. He was the fourth child of John Drawbaugh, a blacksmith, and his wife Leah (née Bloser). The little hamlet was known as Milltown, a mile west of New Cumberland along the Yellow Breeches Creek, on the west shore of the Susquehanna River, opposite Harrisburg. With the rise of the postal service, Milltown was renamed Eberly's Mills.

John and Leah had met in western Cumberland County, near Bloserville, where William Drawbaugh, Daniel's grandfather, was a blacksmith and farmer. The elder Drawbaugh had lived for a time at Eberly's Mills before moving to Bloserville in 1811. Also in the area was a skilled carpenter named Peter Bloser, Leah's father. After William died in 1817, his son John took up his trade and soon moved his family back to

Daniel Drawbaugh

Eberly's Mills. John and Leah had six children: John, Elizabeth, Rebecca, Daniel, Henry, and Catherine.

John Drawbaugh, beyond his ordinary smithing, made edged tools, gun barrels, and other special orders. His brother George was a wagonmaker nearby. A tinkerer with the inherited mechanical skills of his forbears, Daniel Drawbaugh was not good at book learning at the county school. He preferred to spend time in the workshop. At a young age, Daniel began assisting his father, who provided a box on which he could stand by the bellows. He also had a strong desire to make mechanical things.

At the schoolhouse at Cedar Grove, he was often distracted. One day, he noticed cold air coming through a small hole in the wall and

Daniel Drawbaugh sitting outside his workshop along the Yellow Breeches near New Cumberland

immediately began thinking about building a miniature windmill. This he did in his spare time. Then, while the other students were absorbed in their books and the teacher was looking away, he rigged the little machine up against the wall. The little contraption sprang into operation but shrieked when doing so, startling the teacher and his classmates.

"What's that?" the teacher asked the class. All eyes turned to Daniel, who confessed. The teacher then asked Daniel to demonstrate his machine and explain how it worked. Afterward, he flogged him.

It was not long until Daniel began converting his labors into income by making more practical things. His boot trees were popular, earning him spending money. By age seventeen, he made a rifle so fine; he was able to sell it for $18. He also made a clock and a steam engine.

When a local farmer mentioned a need for a mowing machine, young Drawbaugh constructed one which functioned until it was damaged in an accident. Another man requested a specialized attachment for his drill, which Daniel manufactured.

By age seventeen, Daniel and his brother John engaged in coach making. It was Daniel who spent many hours upgrading the machinery they were using. While this improved the process, it was clear Daniel was less interested in the coaches they were producing. He fell back to tinkering and inventing, creating many appliances he did not patent promptly due to a lack of funds and a sponsor. In 1851, Daniel filed for his first patent for a stave jointing machine. Patent number 8505 was issued to him.

On January 1, 1854, Daniel Drawbaugh married Elsetta Thompson, the daughter of local politician John Thompson and his wife, Mary. The couple settled in at Daniel's boyhood home at Eberly's Mills. They had four children who survived well into adulthood, including Iola, Bella, Maud, and Charles. Seven others died young, though Emma lived long enough to marry William Sheely and produce a son, Roy Sheely.

While Daniel wasn't fathering children, he could be found in his workshop in the unused clover mill, which was situated on a peninsula between the Cedar Run and Yellow Breeches Creek. There he repaired clocks, mended tools, and devised inventions. Guests also enjoyed tinkering with him or the turkey shoots on the lawn and Saturday night games of "seven-up." During these years, he patented a stave machine, millstones, and a machine for leveling them. In 1865, he patented a nail plate feeder. The following year, he patented a measuring faucet.

Around 1867, among his many contraptions, Drawbaugh began demonstrating a device that could convey the human voice via electric current over a wire. He continued to experiment with the design and make improvements, but he did not patent it due to a lack of funds. He also did not keep precise records and did not control the rodents that had infested the old mill, often getting into and ruining his wares in short order.

No one had suggested that Daniel protect his invention, and many believed it a waste of time. When he boasted to the village undertaker, William Darr, that he could converse over a wire "across the ocean," Darr scoffed that he should try it first across the Yellow Breeches. Drawbaugh's brother ridiculed his talking machine as a "foolish invention that would amount to nothing." He reminded Daniel he had a large family to raise. Daniel's wife hounded him and even smashed his photographic equipment to "stop him from fooling around with them." Photography was a hobby of Drawbaugh's.

In 1876, Alexander Graham Bell was awarded a patent on the critical components of the telephone. In 1878, Bell's partners organized the Bell American Telephone Company and were soon deluged with patent challenges in the courts led by telegraphy behemoth, the Western Union Company. Western Union challenged Bell with designs acquired from Edison, Dolbear, Gray, and others, but could not defeat Bell in court. Ultimately, they settled in 1879.

In 1880, the Bell company sued an upstart named the Peoples Telephone Company in New York, which had purchased the designs of Daniel Drawbaugh, expecting to defeat the challenger quickly. Drawbaugh claimed that he had invented the telephone nearly ten years before Bell but had not been able to patent it until the present time. Patent law permitted the backdating of the patent to the point when the invention was first successfully demonstrated rather than the date of patent filing. Drawbaugh's neighbors were called as witnesses and confirmed that they had heard muffled words through his device in 1866 or 1867. During the lengthy case, nearly 400 witnesses were summoned, and over 1200 pages of testimony were recorded.

Bell's lawyers painted Drawbaugh as a charlatan and pointed out he had visited the Centennial Exhibition in Philadelphia, and having heard about Bell's invention, said nothing of his own at that time. Also, Drawbaugh did not help his cause when he testified, "I don't remember how I came to it. I had been experimenting in that direction. I don't remember of getting at it by accident either. I don't remember of anyone talking to me of it."

Many of Drawbaugh's components demonstrated at the trial were not his originals, having been damaged by rodents or wear and tear. He was permitted to reconstruct them from memory since he did not have good records. His devices were tested for hours, as were Bells. Both worked, but Drawbaugh's were finicky and required more intervention to keep working.

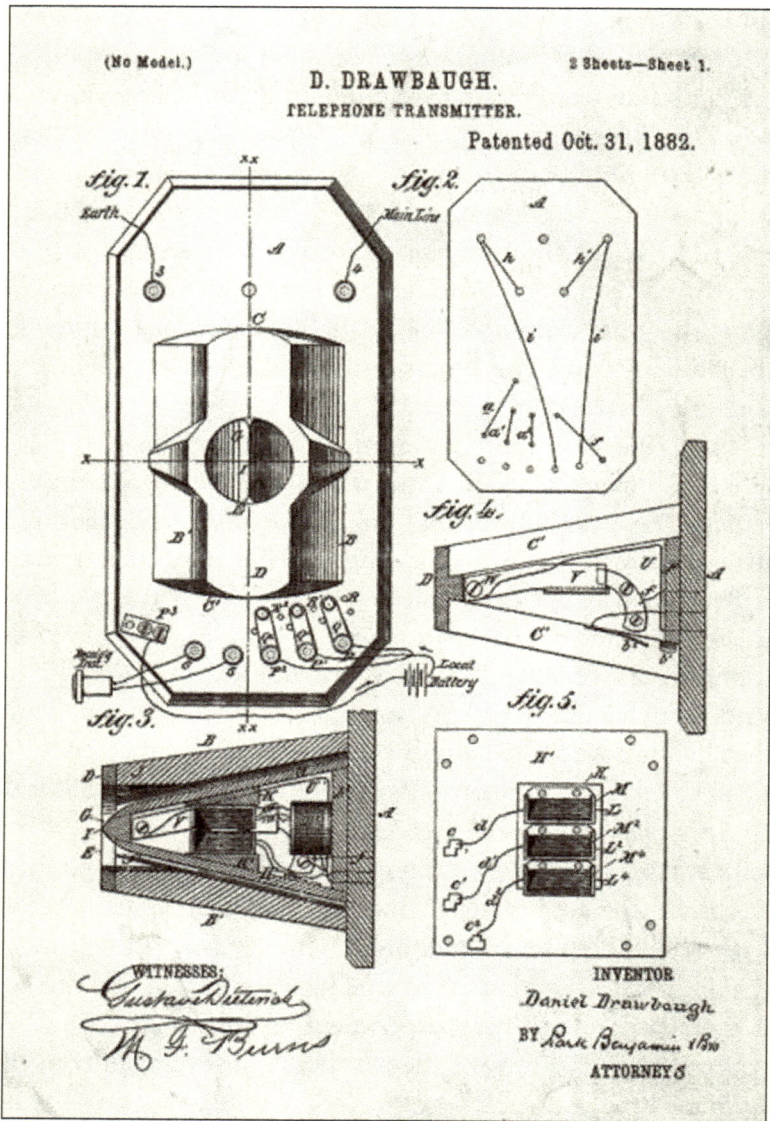

Daniel Drawbaugh's telephone patent

The case dragged on for seven years, including appeals that took it to the U.S. Supreme Court in 1888. There, only seven of the nine justices heard the case and five other telephone-related cases. Justice Horace

Gray recused himself when it was revealed a family member had a large stake in Bell company stock. The recently appointed Lucius Lamar was absent because he was too new to the case. On March 19, 1888, Chief Justice Morrison Waite wrote for the narrow 4 to 3 majority ruling against Drawbaugh. Justices Joseph Bradley, John Marshall Harlan, and Stephen Johnson Field agreed with Drawbaugh. Waite, Stanley Matthews, William Woods, and Samuel Blatchford voted against Drawbaugh. Some newspapers reported one of the justices in the majority could have gone either way. Drawbaugh suspected another justice of bias, as a holder of significant amounts of Bell stock. Chief Justice Waite passed away unexpectedly from pneumonia less than a week after the ruling, and it was Blatchford who read the findings in court on March 25. In summary, the dissenters noted overwhelming evidence from witnesses that Drawbaugh's invention predated Bell's. The slim majority found Bell to have the better claim, focusing more on Bell's patent filing. Drawbaugh continued his fight against Bell to no avail. Peoples Telephone went out of business soon after.

Throughout the 1880s, Drawbaugh patented over a dozen improvements to the telephone as well as a magnetic clock and a braiding machine. Further telephone improvements and pneumatic tools were the focus of his patents during the 1890s. All along, Drawbaugh kept up the fight with Bell, believing he had invented the telephone first.

In 1903, Drawbaugh gained national attention again when he claimed he had invented a method for the wireless transmission of sound, in effect radio, years before Marconi. Drawbaugh claimed he had been experimenting with the technology as early as the 1880s and that he could transmit wirelessly over four miles. Not much came of the claim except an attempt on his life.

Late one night in May 1903, Mrs. Drawbaugh awoke to find a man standing over her husband with a pillow in his hands, about to snuff out the inventor. She shrieked, and the man fled as the rest of the house awoke. The intruder joined two others on the road and ran out of the village as gunshots followed them, all missing. Daniel was found to be drugged but soon recovered. Two nights later, someone tried to burn down the Drawbaugh house, but the village fire brigade rescued it, and no one was hurt.

Daniel suspected someone was after him for the wireless invention. Unfortunately, no insurance company would now back the Drawbaugh property for fear he was a target. He patented his method of wireless transmission in 1904 despite the risk.

In 1911, Drawbaugh filed patents for his final inventions, two versions of a coin sorter to be used by bank tellers. On November 2, at age 84, he died of a stroke in his workshop while working on a wireless burglar alarm.

Daniel Drawbaugh was laid to rest in St. John's Cemetery near Shiremanstown, Cumberland County. Had just one more Supreme Court Justice voted in the affirmative rather than the negative, the history books would have changed, and we would all be talking about the Peoples Telephone Company rather than Bell's. Drawbaugh would have likely died a wealthy man with a lot more than the paltry $350 left to his heirs.

The grave of Daniel Drawbaugh

9.

ROBERT BUDD DWYER

"An Innocent Man?"

County: Crawford • Town: Blooming Valley
Buried at Blooming Valley Cemetery
Blooming Valley

He was born in Missouri but attended college and eventually settled in Pennsylvania. He began his career as a high school teacher before deciding to enter the political world and run for a seat in the Pennsylvania State Assembly. He eventually won multiple elections to both the state house and the state senate. He then successfully made two bids for the statewide office of Pennsylvania treasurer. In the mid-1980s, the United States Justice Department investigated him for corruption relating to the acceptance of a bribe in return for awarding a state contract. He was indicted and found guilty on eleven counts. On the day before he was to go before a judge to be sentenced, he called a press conference at which many believed he would announce his resignation. Instead, he read a statement, again maintaining his innocence, pulled a .357 Magnum revolver from an envelope, inserted the weapon in his mouth, and pulled the trigger. The public suicide was broadcast later that day by many Pennsylvania television stations. His full name was Robert Budd Dwyer, but virtually all referred to him and knew him as Budd Dwyer.

Dwyer was born on November 21, 1939, in St. Charles, Missouri. He came to Pennsylvania to attend college and eventually made the Keystone State his home. After earning a master's degree in education, he became a teacher at Cambridge Springs High School, where he taught social studies and coached football. It was during this period he married another high school teacher, Joanne Grappy. The couple had two children.

Dwyer entered the political world when he was elected as a Republican to the State House of Representatives. He won re-election to his House seat in 1966 and 1968. In 1970 he successfully ran for a seat in the Pennsylvania Senate. He was then re-elected to the Senate in 1974 and 1978. In 1980 he decided to run for the statewide office of Pennsylvania treasurer.

Dwyer took on an incumbent state treasurer in the 1980 election. Democrat Robert E. Casey had been elected to the post in 1976 and was looking for a second term. Casey had been an obscure Cambria County official before his win in the 1976 race. His win has often been credited to the fact that many thought they were voting for a future Pennsylvania governor, Robert P. Casey (See *Keystone Tombstones Volume Three*). Robert P. was a well-known state politician who had served in the state senate, made three unsuccessful runs for governor, and had been elected auditor general twice. In the 1980 race, Dwyer made it a point to let voters know that his opponent was not the real Robert P. Casey. On election night, Dwyer emerged victorious by a margin of 70,073 votes.

From 1979 to 1981, before Dwyer began his service as the state treasurer, public employees in Pennsylvania had overpaid millions of dollars in Federal Insurance Contributions Act taxes. As a result, the commonwealth needed an accounting firm to determine what refunds should be provided to the employees. Dwyer awarded the no-bid contract to perform this function to Computer Technology Associates (CTA), a firm based in California owned by John Torquato, Jr., a Pennsylvania native. The contract was estimated to be worth between two to five million dollars. Dwyer would later say that the contract was awarded to CTA because the company pledged to bring at least twenty-five new jobs to Pennsylvania and because the company had experience in similar recovery projects. This contract would become the subject of a federal investigation that would include the FBI and federal prosecutors.

When Dwyer took office as treasurer, the governor of Pennsylvania was Richard Thornburgh. Though both Dwyer and Thornburgh were

The tragic final seconds of Budd Dwyer

Republicans, their relationship was rocky due to two events that the press brought to the attention of the public. First, Dwyer refused to pay a travel voucher submitted by the governor's wife, Ginny Thornburgh, to cover airfare for a trade mission to Germany and England. Dwyer said that the law and management directives simply didn't cover travel expenses for the families of state officials. The governor's office accused Dwyer of taking a cheap shot and added that the bill would be paid. The governor and the treasurer butted heads again when Dwyer learned that Thornburgh was using state police troopers to transport two of his sons to school in Massachusetts. Dwyer sent a letter to the State Police Commissioner suggesting that some of the nearly $7,000 in costs was for transportation and not security and that Thornburgh should reimburse the state for any costs not related to security. The governor defended the use of the state troopers as something "entirely proper." After these run-ins, Dwyer was convinced that Thornburgh was out to get him.

It was after these two events that Thornburgh received an anonymous memo alleging bribery had occurred during the awarding of the state contract to CTA. The matter was referred to the FBI, who began an investigation. When news of this investigation reached Dwyer, he canceled the CTA contract on July 11, 1984. However, this didn't halt the investigation. Federal officials charged Dwyer with agreeing to receive a kickback of $300,000 in exchange for awarding the contract to CTA. The Justice Department also indicted Torquato, his attorney William T. Smith, and Smith's wife. Attorney Smith proved to be a key witness in the case.

During the trials and through the years, Smith's accounts surrounding the awarding of the contract have changed. Four days after being indicted, Smith claimed that Torquato insisted that he offer Dwyer $300,000 if he signed a contract with CTA. Smith said he made such an offer to Dwyer during a meeting in the treasurer's office. Smith said Dwyer was receptive to the idea and talked about splitting the money three ways with thirds going to him personally, to his campaign, and the Republican State Committee. Smith also claimed that Dwyer said he would talk to Robert Asher, the Republican Party Chairman for Pennsylvania, to inquire about how this business should be conducted.

The story continued with Smith's account of a conversation with Asher, who said he had discussed the matter with Dwyer. He described Asher as objecting to the split and recalled that the Chairman was angry that any such offer had been made directly to Dwyer. Asher indicated that if there was going to be a contribution, the entire amount would go to the Republican State Committee.

However, the following year when Smith was brought to trial, he claimed that it was Torquato who made the offer of a campaign contribution to Dwyer and that Dwyer rejected it. Torquato testified that it was Smith who made the offer. Dwyer, a witness for the defense, testified that he was never offered any contribution from either Torquato or Smith. Smith was convicted and sentenced to twelve years in prison. On May 13, 1986, a grand jury indicted both Dwyer and Asher. Hoping for a reduction in his sentence, Smith agreed to testify on behalf of the federal government against Dwyer and Asher. While he received no such reduction, his wife, Judy Smith, was granted immunity from prosecution. When Dwyer and Asher were brought to trial, Smith went back to his original story. In 2010 the documentary *Honest Man: The Life of R. Budd*

Dwyer was released. Smith appeared in the film and said, "To the day I die, I'll regret that I did it." He also said, "He's dead because of me."

The lead federal prosecutor in the case was United States Attorney James West. West had the reputation of being a thorough, competent, and aggressive prosecutor. He and his team put forth a case that established that Dwyer had lobbied for the approval of the legislation that authorized him to recover the overpayments. They produced a computer tape seized from CTA that showed that Dwyer was to receive $300,000 for giving CTA the contract. They also had the testimony of both Smith and Torquato. They produced another witness, Charles Collins, who had served as a Director of Management Consulting for Arthur Young and Associates, a Pennsylvania-based accounting firm. Collins testified that Arthur Young and Associates was ready to negotiate a contract for half the cost of the CTA contract and that Dwyer was aware of this before awarding the work to CTA. Dwyer maintained that he had awarded the contract based on a recommendation of his task force. He denied any wrongdoing and said Smith had merely made a general offer to help him with his campaign.

At his trial, Dwyer did not testify, nor did his lawyer, Paul Killion, present any witnesses because he felt the government had failed to prove its case. On December 18, 1986, the jury found both Dwyer and Asher guilty. Dwyer had been found guilty on eleven counts of conspiracy, mail fraud, perjury, and interstate transportation in aid of racketeering. He faced a sentence of up to 55 years in prison and a $300,000 fine. One of the jurors said that she had found it emotionally challenging to convict both Dwyer and Asher since they were men "of very high integrity . . . they had just made a mistake." It is worth noting that no money from CTA was ever given to Dwyer or the State Republican Party. The prosecution successfully argued that showing the intent to accept the offer of a bribe was enough to convict. James West never questioned the outcome of the trial. Years later, he told a Harrisburg reporter, "Is there a shadow of doubt in my mind that he was guilty? No. He was guilty." Not all of Pennsylvania's government officials agreed with West. Democrat Senator

Mark Singel, who had been elected the commonwealth's lieutenant governor during the trial, would come to characterize the Dwyer conviction as a complete miscarriage of justice, adding, "I think this was a man who was tragically destroyed by forces that were more mendacious than he was."

Judge Malcolm Muir scheduled Dwyer's sentencing for January 23, 1987. Dwyer refused to resign as state treasurer and scheduled a news conference in the state's Finance Building for the day before. Most people and the press who attended the conference expected Dwyer to announce his resignation. Attorney West said that the resignation "sounds like the appropriate thing to do under the circumstances." A Harrisburg reporter said that the consensus among those attending was they were being called to witness a resignation. The evening before the conference, Dwyer wrote a note stating, "I enjoy being with Jo so much, the next twenty years or so would have been wonderful. Tomorrow is going to be difficult, and I hope I can go through with it."

Appearing at the conference, Dwyer was described as nervous and agitated. He read from a 21-page prepared text. His remarks contained criticisms of Attorney West, Judge Muir, and particularly of Governor Dick Thornburgh, whom he described as having a short temper and a vicious, vindictive personality. He added that Thornburgh was out to get him because of the decisions he had made relative to the reimbursements for the governor's wife and sons. He claimed that Thornburgh referred to him as "the fat fuck" and that a member of the Thornburgh cabinet upon learning of the CTA investigation remarked that "the fat fuck is going to get it now." The speech lasted for thirty minutes, and when he got to the last page, he stopped reading the prepared remarks. Dwyer then handed out three envelopes to members of his staff. One contained a letter to Pennsylvania's new governor, Bob Casey, who had taken office two days before. One contained an organ donor card. The last contained three letters: one each to his wife and children as well as suggested funeral arrangements. At this point, he opened a large manila envelope and pulled out a Smith and Wesson Model 27 .357 Magnum revolver. Many in the room gasped as Dwyer backed up against the wall said, "Please, please leave the room if this will upset you." As some in the room pleaded with him to stop and others began to approach him, he said his final words,

"Don't, don't, don't this will hurt someone. Sit down." He then inserted the revolver into his mouth and fired a shot that entered his brain, killing him instantly. He fell to the floor gun still in hand.

The final page of Dwyer's prepared remarks, which he never delivered, read as follows. "I've repeatedly said that I'm not going to resign as state treasurer. After many hours of thought and meditation, I've made a decision that should not be an example to anyone because it is unique to my situation. Last May I told you that after the trial, I would give you the story of the decade. To those of you who are shallow, the events of this morning will be that story. But for those of you with depth and concern, the real story will be what I hope and pray results from this morning—in the coming months and years, the development of a true justice system here in the United States. I am going to die in office to see if the shameful facts spread out in all their shame, will not burn through our civic shamelessness and set fire to American pride. Please tell my story on every radio and television station and in every newspaper and magazine in the U.S. Please leave immediately if you have a weak stomach or mind since I don't want to cause physical or mental distress. Joanne, Rob, DeeDee, I love you! Thank you for making my life so happy. Goodbye to you all on the count of three. Please make sure that the sacrifice of my life is not in vain."

A good portion of the public viewed Dwyer's public suicide as an admission of guilt. They viewed his act as that of a man looking to avoid prison. However, there may have been another motive. If Dwyer had been sentenced, state law would have prohibited the payment of his pension benefits. Because he died in office, his widow was able to collect survivor benefits, which totaled over $1.28 million. At the time, it was the largest death benefit ever awarded by the state retirement system. Statements made by his family and friends support the latter as having motivated Dwyer's suicide.

Almost a thousand people filed past Dwyer's state-flag-draped casket before his funeral and burial as he lay in a Meadville area funeral home. There was also a memorial service held for him in Hershey. Those attending the memorial service included United States Senator Arlen Specter (See *Keystone Tombstones Volume Three*), Pennsylvania's former Lt. Governor William W. Scranton III, and the commonwealth's recently elected Lt. Governor, Mark Singel. The authors spoke to Singel and asked if he could share his thoughts on Dwyer. Singel recalled receiving a note from Dwyer a few days before his own inauguration and just before the fatal news conference. In the note, Dwyer told Singel he had always respected him and knew he would do great things for the people of Pennsylvania and have a positive impact for years to come. He added that he was sorry he wouldn't be around to see it. At the time, Singel felt that Dwyer was referring to his upcoming prison sentence. In light of subsequent events, he now sees that message differently. When asked what he thought about Dwyer and the CTA episode, Singel was succinct, "Budd Dwyer didn't have a criminal bone in his body."

Dwyer was laid to rest in Blooming Valley Cemetery near Meadville beneath a keystone-shaped tombstone that details his service to the people of Pennsylvania.

The grave of Budd Dwyer, a real keystone tombstone

10.

ENOCH BROWN (1694–1764) AND RUTH HALE, RUTH HART, EBEN TAYLOR, GEORGE DUSTAN, TWO DEAN BOYS, AND FOUR UNKNOWNS

"America's First School Massacre"

County: Franklin • Town: Antrim Township
Buried at Enoch Brown Memorial Park
2730 Enoch Brown Road

In a bucolic wooded park in rural Antrim Township, Franklin County, Pennsylvania, northwest of Greencastle, stands a solitary gray granite obelisk honoring a deceased schoolmaster and ten of his pupils lost in a horrific mass murder committed by members of the Delaware tribe in the months after the French and Indian War during a conflict known as Pontiac's War. It was the first mass murder in a school in what would become the United States of America.

The French and Indian War had ended with the Treaty of Paris in February 1763. However, tensions remained high in Penn's colony between the natives and the white settlers, especially as the Scotch-Irish continued to settle into the western reaches of the commonwealth, outside of the territorial limits agreed to in treaties.

Later that year, in December, the infamous Paxton Boys massacred over twenty Conestoga Indians, including women and children, who had

The horrific murder of the Conestogas by the Paxton Boys near Lancaster, Pennsylvania

been living peacefully near Lancaster. This was in response to attacks occurring in the wilderness and a general lack of trust between the two sides.

William Henry, from Lancaster, witnessed the attack:

> I saw a number of people running down the street towards
> the gaol, which enticed me and other lads to follow them. At
> about sixty or eighty yards from the gaol, we met from twenty-
> five to thirty men, well mounted on horses, and with rifles,
> tomahawks, and scalping knives, equipped for murder. I ran
> into the prison yard, and there, O what a horrid sight presented
> itself to my view! Near the back door of the prison, lay an old
> Indian and his women, particularly well-known and esteemed
> by the people of the town, on account of his placid and friendly
> conduct. His name was Will Sock; across him and his Native
> women lay two children, of about the age of three years, whose
> heads were split with the tomahawk, and their scalps all taken
> off. Towards the middle of the gaol yard, along the west side

68

of the wall, lay a stout Indian, whom I particularly noticed to have been shot in the breast, his legs were chopped with the tomahawk, his hands cut off, and finally, a rifle ball discharged in his mouth; so that his head was blown to atoms, and the brains were splashed against, and yet hanging to the wall, for three or four feet around. This man's hands and feet had also been chopped off with a tomahawk. In this manner lay the whole of them, men, women, and children, spread about the prison yard: shot-scalped-hacked-and cut to pieces.

When 250 Paxton Boys marched on Philadelphia in January 1764 to demand action by the government and to attack over 150 Indians hiding there, Benjamin Franklin and other civic leaders met with them. Said Franklin at the time ". . . the Conestoga would have been safe among any other people on earth, no matter how primitive, except white savages from Peckstang and Donegall!" Embarrassed, the Paxton Boys dispersed.

Throughout the year, tensions simmered, and attacks flared on the edges of the wilderness. Finally bending to pressure from the settlers, on July 7, 1764, John Penn, the governor and grandson of William Penn, signed a decree offering a bounty for Indian scalps:

For every male Indian enemy above ten years old, who shall be taken prisoner and delivered at any forts garrisoned by the troops in pay of this Province, or at any of the county towns, to the keeper of the common gaols there, the sum of one hundred & fifty Spanish dollars, or pieces of eight; for every female enemy taken prisoner and brought in as aforesaid, and for every male Indian enemy ten years old, or under, taken prisoner, and delivered as aforesaid, the sum of one hundred & thirty pieces of eight; for the scalp of every male Indian enemy above the age of ten years, produced as evidence of their being killed, the sum of one hundred & thirty pieces of eight, and for the scalp of every female Indian enemy above the age of ten years, produced

The Paxton Boys march on Philadelphia to demand action and to attack Indians harbored there

as evidence of their being killed, the sum of fifty pieces of eight; and that there shall be paid to every officer, or officers, soldier, or soldiers, as are or shall be in the pay of this Province, who shall take, bring in, and produce any Indian enemy prisoner, or scalp, as aforesaid, one half of said several and respective premiums & bounties.

The Pennsylvania Archives record "secret expeditions" following the decree that were "more effective than any sort of defensive operations."

Less than three weeks later, on July 26, 1764, a small war party of four or more Delawares approached the settlements in Antrim Township. They came upon Susan King Cunningham, on the road on her way to a neighbor's house. She was with child. The Indians beat her to death, scalped her, and cut the unborn baby from her body, setting it next to her.

The party then turned its attention to a log cabin in which Enoch Brown, the schoolmaster, was conducting a class for eleven of his students. Fortunately, several students did not attend that day for various reasons. Enoch, who had been born in Ireland and was approaching his 70th birthday, was a pious man and one of the few teachers in the region. When the war party entered the cabin, Brown offered himself provided the children would be spared. The Indians would hear none of it, and while at least two guarded the door, the third proceeded to murder and scalp all present. From *Notes on Franklin County History* by John L. Finafrock:

> One of the cherished traditions of the terrible tragedy is that Schoolmaster Brown was shot down with the Bible in his hand before he could make any resistance and on his knees begged only that the innocent children might be spared. Parkman, in describing the ghastly sight that met those who first entered the schoolhouse after the massacre, says: 'In the center lay the master, scalped and lifeless, with a Bible clasped in his hands; while around the room were strewn the bodies of his mangled pupils.' Another tradition says that Mr. Linn, while working in a meadow in the vicinity, heard the shot that killed Schoolmaster Brown, and when he and others came to see what was the matter they found little Archie McCullough, who survived the scalping, sitting by the spring nearby washing the blood from his mangled head. He told them that when the four Indians opened the door, Master Brown, knowing well their object begged them to take him as their victim and let the innocent children return to their homes. The same instant he was shot down, and then he and the other children were quickly tomahawked and scalped by two of the savages while the other two stood with murderous weapons in the doorway.

The local farmers were horrified. The bodies of the children were initially returned to their families and taken to their homes. Several days

The obelisk marking the spot of the former Enoch Brown cabin where the massacre occurred

later, Enoch Brown and his students were laid to rest together in a large wooden box and buried near the schoolhouse. Most accounts say ten students were killed. Ruth Hale, Ruth Hart, Eben Taylor, George Dustan, two Dean boys, and four unknowns are listed among the dead. Some accounts say one child other than Archie survived the scalping. One account adds that four additional children were captured.

One of the four inscriptions on the obelisk

When the war party returned home to their camp at Muskingum in the Ohio Country and showed-off their scalps, they were ostracized by their chief. John McCullough, a young settler and cousin of Archie who had been captured years before and was a prisoner, witnessed the arrival of the warriors and wrote in his diary:

> I saw the Indians when they returned home with the scalps;
> some of the old Indians were very much displeased at them
> for killing so many children, especially Neep-paugh'-whese,
> or Night Walker, an old chief, or half king—he ascribed it to
> cowardice, which was the greatest affront he could offer them.

According to tradition, some of the children had hesitated to go to school that day. Only eleven, two girls and nine boys were present, representing ten families.

One of the absentees was Sarah "Sally" Brown, the daughter of George Brown of Brown's Mill. She remained home to assist the family with pulling flax. Later, she married Benjamin Chambers, the son of the founder of Chambersburg and a Lieutenant in the Revolutionary War.

Elenore Cochran, who was from Waynesboro, was living with the George Brown family to attend school with Sally. She also stayed home that day. She later married Captain Joseph Junkins, who became a hero in the Revolution. Of their fourteen children, Elenore was the first wife of General Stonewall Jackson.

Elenore Pawling, whose father operated the Pawling Tavern, remained home that day. She ultimately married Dr. Robert Johnston, a distinguished surgeon during the Revolutionary War.

Mary Ramsey had a premonition that some evil was going to happen and stayed home. She later married into the Agnew family, who were in the medical profession. Her niece, Mary, married Archibald Irvin. One of their daughters, Jane, married the son of President William Henry Harrison. As a widow in 1841, she was the mistress of the White House during her father-in-law's brief administration. Jane's sister, Elizabeth, married John Scott Harrison, also a son of the president. They became the parents of Benjamin Harrison, who was the twenty-third president of the United States.

James Poe played hooky that day. A neighbor, Mrs. Betty Hopkins, saw James climb a tree to watch a local farmer mow his hay. When he returned home, he lied about going to school and was punished. James later served in the militia and rose to captain during the Revolution. He was involved in local government and politics for many years.

For many years, this tale was thought to be legendary. The gravesite was unmarked, and many of the families had moved away. Widow Betty Hopkins, who lived in a small house near the school, had her windows covered with wooden boards giving the appearance that the house was abandoned. The war party passed her by that day, but she vividly recalled the burial of the unfortunates and repeated the story to David Detrich as a boy. He later became General David Detrich, who laid Mrs. Hopkins to rest at the age of 104 in the 1840s. Detrich recalled the story of the schoolhouse scalpings and worked with community member Andrew

The nearby grave of Enoch Brown and ten schoolchildren

Rankin to investigate it. Rankin and twenty citizens of the area dug at the location to try to rediscover the burial site. They were successful, unearthing the skeletons of one adult and ten children in a common grave. At the time, the landowner, Christian Hoser, planted four locust trees to mark the site.

When the trees were cut down in the spring of 1883, some locals felt the site would be forgotten if something wasn't done. The following year, the Franklin County Centennial Convention decided to raise money to honor Enoch Brown and the children with a park and a monument on the site of the former cabin. It was dedicated in 1885 inscribed with information about the fallen and the following:

The ground is holy where they fell
And where their mingled ashes lie,
Ye Christian people mark it well
With granite column strong and high;

And cherish well, forevermore,
The storied wealth of early years,
The sacred legacies of yore
The toils and trials of pioneers.

The nearby gravesite was also marked with a monument inscribed: "The gravesite of Enoch Brown and ten scholars massacred by the Indians July 26, 1764. In 1998, a third monument was erected by the creek, down the hill from the grave. It honors the Archie McCullough

The plaque marking the spot where Archie McCullough washed his bloody head

spring, where the children would go for water and where Archie washed his bloody scalp.

Remembrances have been held at the site over the years, and a coin was struck by the Greencastle Rotary Club in 1964, upon the 200th anniversary.

Today, quaint little Enoch Brown park is tucked between residences along Enoch Brown Road. There is a children's playground on the site and a short hiking trail in addition to the monuments.

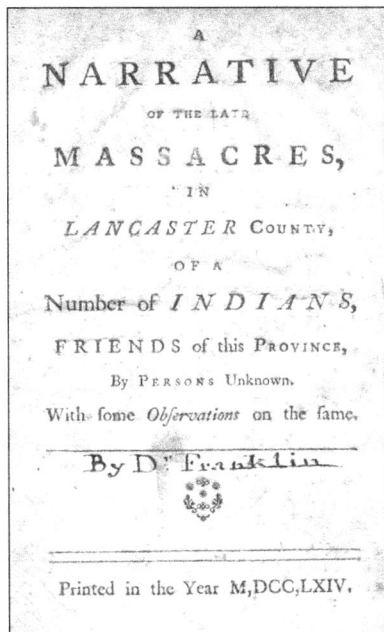

A

NARRATIVE

OF THE LATE

MASSACRES,

IN

LANCASTER COUNTY,

OF A

Number of INDIANS,

FRIENDS of this PROVINCE,

By PERSONS Unknown.

With some Observations on the same.

By Dr Franklin

Printed in the Year M,DCC,LXIV.

Ben Franklin's pamphlet regarding the Paxton Boys

II.

HENRY CLAY FRICK

"Coke Baron"

County: Allegheny • Town: Pittsburgh
Buried at The Homewood Cemetery
1599 South Dallas Avenue

Henry Clay Frick made a fortune providing the fuel for the steel furnaces of Pittsburgh during the Gilded Age. His partnership with Andrew Carnegie led to him becoming chairman of the Carnegie Steel Company and then played a role in the formation of the U.S. Steel conglomerate. At one point, one of the wealthiest men in America, he also financed other businesses and built an impressive collection of fine art.

Henry Clay Frick was born on December 18, 1849, in West Overton, Westmoreland County, Pennsylvania, a descendant of German Mennonites. His father, John W. Frick (1822–1888), was a modest businessman and farmer. His mother, Elizabeth Stauffer Overholt Frick (1819–1905), was the daughter of a prosperous merchant and distiller, Abraham Overholt. His brand of spirit, Old Overholt, is touted as America's oldest continually maintained brand of whiskey to this day. Abraham's father, a Mennonite named Henry Oberholzer, founded the company in 1810 after he settled in Westmoreland County, on the banks of the Jacobs Creek.

Frick was exposed to the workings of the distillery business at a young age. He was sent to Otterbein College for a year but did not graduate. He then worked for a time as a salesman in Pittsburgh before becoming the bookkeeper for the distillery.

Henry Clay Frick

In 1871, Frick, two cousins, and a friend formed a partnership to purchase coal mines and then made coke out of bituminous coal by heating it to the point where its gases and tars are removed. Coke was the fuel for steel manufacturing, a burgeoning business in the area. The company was called the Frick Coke Company, and Frick vowed to be a millionaire by the end of the decade. During the financial panic of 1873, the cash-rich company thrived and acquired more properties.

By 1880, with the help of his lifelong friend Andrew W. Mellon, Frick controlled eighty percent of the coke used by Pittsburgh's steel industry, operating primarily in Westmoreland and Fayette Counties. Frick used loans from the Mellons to buy out his partners and establish H. C. Frick & Company, employing over 1,000 workers. He had become a millionaire, and his company operated 12,000 coke ovens and owned 40,000 acres of coal.

Early in 1881, Frick took over his late grandfather's distillery. He split ownership evenly with Andrew Mellon and Charles Mauck. The company, now headquartered in Pittsburgh, remained a sentimental side business for Frick throughout his life.

As a wealthy young man in his early thirties, Frick moved to Pittsburgh and married twenty-two-year-old Adelaide Howard Childs, the daughter of a boot and shoe manufacturer, in December 1881. The two settled in the Homewood section of the city and purchased an Italianate eleven-room mansion called Clayton. The couple had four children, but only two survived to adulthood. A son, Childs, was born in 1883, and a daughter, Helen, was born in 1888. Clayton was later expanded, in 1891, into twenty-three rooms.

While the Fricks were on their honeymoon in New York in early 1882, Henry met Andrew Carnegie, who had been one of his largest customers. By May, Frick and Carnegie forged a partnership with Frick gaining eleven percent of Carnegie Steel while Carnegie gained a controlling interest in H. C. Frick & Company. This arrangement assured Carnegie that he would have ample coke for his operations at a reasonable price. Frick was further enriched and was elevated to chairman of the Carnegie company when Carnegie retired in 1889. The relationship was complicated at times, with Carnegie trying to force Frick out of the business and disregarding many of his decisions. Regardless, Frick dedicated himself to the success and growth of their companies, fueled by the rapid expansion of the railroads.

The attempted assassination of Henry Clay Frick

During these successful years, Frick, at the suggestion of his friend, Benjamin Ruff, helped to found the South Fork Fishing and Hunting Club near Johnstown, Pennsylvania. This elite organization included among its members Frick's best friend, Andrew Mellon, his attorneys Philadander Knox and James Hay Reed, and Andrew Carnegie. In all, more than sixty of the most prominent men of the area used the club for recreation away from the spewing smokestacks of the Steel City.

On the expansive property was Lake Conemaugh created by the then world's largest earthen dam, less than twenty miles above Johnstown. Daniel Morrell, who owned the Cambria Iron Company in Johnstown, was concerned about the safety of the dam and sent his engineer, John Fulton, to inspect it. However, little was done, and the matter faded after Morrell died in 1885.

After more years of neglect, due to unusually high snowmelt and heavy spring rains, the dam gave way on May 31, 1889, resulting in the infamous Johnstown Flood that wiped away 2,209 lives and caused millions of dollars in damage.

When Frick and the others learned of the catastrophe, they gathered to start the Pittsburgh Relief Committee to assist the victims. They also vowed never to speak publicly about the club or the flood. Knox and Reed fended off all lawsuits that tried to pin the blame on the club or its members. An investigation by the American Society of Civil Engineers produced a report in 1891, but it was largely whitewashed of any blame.

In 1892, in response to declining prices for steel products, Frick sought to consolidate the various holdings to form the Carnegie Steel Company, creating the largest steel company in the world valued at $25 million. Frick remained at the head of the organization and sought to further protect profits by reducing the wages of his workers.

That summer, the Amalgamated Iron and Steel Workers Union struck in protest. Frick responded by hiring 300 strikebreakers from outside the area and the Pinkerton Detective Agency to protect them and management. Frick ordered the construction of a fence topped by barbed wire around the mill property. The picketing workers dubbed it "Fort Frick." As the armed Pinkertons arrived on barges on the Monongahela River, strikers waited and attacked. A day-long battle ensured resulting

Galley inside the Frick mansion

in the deaths of seven Pinkertons and nine workers before Pennsylvania Governor Robert Pattison placed Homestead under martial law and called in 8,000 state militia under Major General George Snowden. Frick was roundly criticized for his insensitive anti-union stance during one of the bitterest labor disputes in U.S. history.

On July 23, 1892, while the strike simmered, an anarchist named Alexander Berkman gained access to Frick by posing as an agent for the strikebreakers. Berkman, armed with a pistol and a steel file, entered Frick's Pittsburgh office and raised his gun. Frick, seeing the threat to his life, rose from his chair while Berkman fired at point-blank range. The bullet nicked Frick's left earlobe, entered his neck at the base of the skull, and lodged in his back, knocking Frick to the floor. Berkman fired again, hitting Frick in the neck. Frick began to bleed profusely. Before Berkman could fire a third shot, Carnegie Steel vice president John Leishman, who was in the room, and Frick both jumped on the assassin. A struggle ensued as the three men thrashed about on the floor, Berkman stabbing Frick several times with the file before he was subdued by other employees who had come to the rescue. Afterward, Frick cabled both his mother and Carnegie: "Was twice shot, but not dangerously."

Though seriously wounded, Frick was back to work within a week. Negative publicity from the assassination attempt toppled the strike, resulting in 2500 men losing their jobs and wages being halved. Berkman was tried and convicted of attempted murder and sentenced to 22 years in prison.

Carnegie was not happy with the labor issues, and the two men struggled to get along over the rest of the decade, though profits grew from $2 million to $40 million annually. Frick became the chairman of the board in December 1894, but five years later, Carnegie abolished his position as chairman, and the two went to court over Frick's interest. Frick won a settlement of $30 million in securities in March 1900 and was effectively out of the partnership with Carnegie. He then proceeded to form the St. Clair Steel Company, operating the most extensive coke works in the world.

Carnegie and Frick continued to lock horns over coke in 1900. Now no longer controlling Frick, Carnegie still wanted lower prices for coke. The two ultimately settled out of court. The following year, Carnegie sold his company to J. P. Morgan as part of the creation of United States Steel Corporation, now the most substantial steel producer in the world. Frick also sold out and became one of the directors of the behemoth. He was also the largest individual railway stockholder in the world.

Now fabulously wealthy in his early fifties, Frick shifted his focus to collecting art and expanding his properties. In 1904, he built a summer estate, a 104-room mansion named Eagle Rock on Boston's North Shore. The building stood until 1969.

Frick's interest in art influenced his move from Pittsburgh to New York City in 1905. He continued to serve on numerous corporate boards while accumulating paintings by such artists as Vermeer, Rembrandt, El Greco, Titian, and Bellini. He housed them at his mansion at 79th and Fifth Avenue.

In 1907, as the temperance movement was gaining in the country, Frick and Mellon removed their names from the distilling license for the Overholt distillery, though they retained ownership.

In 1910, Frick purchased a private railroad car from the Pullman Company dubbed the *Westmoreland*. It cost nearly $40,000 and provided many of the luxuries of home, including a kitchen, pantry, dining room, servant's quarters, two staterooms, and a lavatory. The Fricks used the car for their frequent travel between his residences in Pittsburgh, New York, and Boston. He also used it for trips to Palm Beach, Florida, and Aiken, South Carolina.

In 1912, Frick and his wife Adelaide were touring Europe and planned to travel back to New York on the maiden voyage of the *Titanic* with J. P. Morgan. Morgan took ill before the trip, and the Fricks canceled when Adelaide sprained her ankle in Italy.

In 1913, construction was started on Frick's mansion between 70th and 71st Streets on Fifth Avenue. The home cost nearly $5 million, including the land, and is a New York landmark to this day. Frick designed

Frick family graves

the house to accommodate his art collection. He intended to leave both the house and the art to the public after his passing.

Henry Clay Frick died of a heart attack on December 2, 1919, only weeks before his 70th birthday. He was laid to rest at Homewood Cemetery in Pittsburgh, Pennsylvania. At a dinner in Chicago, his former would-be assassin, Alexander Berkman, was celebrating his pending deportation to Russia. A reporter asked him what he thought of the sudden passing of Frick. "He has been deported by God," said the anarchist.

In his will, Frick left his house, art, and furnishing to become a gallery called The Frick Collection, subject to the accommodation of his widow. He provided an endowment of $15 million to maintain the gallery and donated nearly $30 million to various charities. He left the whiskey company to his friend, Andrew Mellon.

Frick bequeathed 150 acres of undeveloped land and $2 million to the City of Pittsburgh to be used as a park. This became Frick Park in 1927. Over the years, money from the trust funded the enlargement of the park to nearly 600 acres.

Frick's widow, Adelaide Howard Childs Frick, passed in 1931. The Frick Collection was opened to the public as a museum in December 1935.

Son Childs Frick was a paleontologist who worked with the American Museum of Natural History for many years. He died in 1965. His children, grandchildren, and great-grandchildren have served as presidents of The Frick Collection, and members of the Board of Trustees.

Daughter Helen Clay Frick never married and founded the Frick Art Reference Library in memory of her father in 1920. She remained its director until 1983. In 1981, she returned to Clayton, where she lived until she died in 1984 at the age of 96. The Pittsburgh family home was renovated and opened to the public in 1990 as the Frick Art and Historical Center.

Frick's extensive business records, including correspondence with many of the leading businessmen of the Gilded Age, are now housed at the University of Pittsburgh Library. The history of the Overholt Distillery is also housed there.

12.

BILLY HEATH

"Survivor of Custer's Last Stand?"

County: Schuylkill • Town: Tamaqua
Buried at Odd Fellows Cemetery
503 West Broad Street

On June 25, 1876, one of America's most renowned Indian fighters, George Armstrong Custer, led the troops under his command on an attack aimed at a large Indian village located near the Little Bighorn River in Montana. Custer devised a plan where he split his twelve companies into three battalions. He placed one of the battalions under the command of Major Marcus Reno and the other under Captain Frederick Benteen. Several soldiers serving under these two men would survive. However, as history has recorded, the approximately 210 men who followed Custer into battle were all killed, including the commanding officer. This story has been told in numerous books and movies. No one who rode with Custer left the battle alive. In a 2003 book written by Vincent J. Genovese titled *Billy Heath: The Man Who Survived Custer's Last Stand,* the author argues that the history books have gotten it wrong and that one of Custer's men survived the battle. That man was named Billy Heath.

Heath was born on May 1, 1848, in Staffordshire, England. Little is known about his life in England. His family, it appears, decided to emigrate to the United States and made the dangerous trip that took weeks and was generally spent below the decks of the wooden vessels of those times. Arriving in America, the family made their home in Schuylkill County, Pennsylvania.

On September 30, 1872, Heath applied for United States citizenship. His father-in-law, Joseph Swansborough, was his sponsor. This application was filed within days of his marriage, so Mr. Swansborough may have made the action a condition to obtaining his daughter's hand in matrimony. Heath and his wife made their home in Girardville, where he, like many of the men living in the area, found work mining anthracite coal. At the time, the coal region in northeastern Pennsylvania was the scene of significant labor unrest and violence. Based on tax re-

Billy Heath

cords, it appears that Heath made a decent living as a miner, and by 1875 his wife had given birth to two sons.

A majority of the miners in the region were Irish Catholics who were exploited and discriminated against by the Protestants who owned the mines and put others who shared their religious affiliation in charge of running them. These owners placed the Irish Catholic miners in poor housing located in company-owned towns and required them to shop only at the company store. As a rule, their wages failed to cover their expenses, and these miners found themselves in debt to the mine owners. As an English Protestant, Heath likely avoided this discrimination and, as we shall see, may have found other avenues of employment available.

As labor unrest grew in the region, the owners contended that it was fueled by a secret society that was known as the Molly Maguires (See *Keystone Tombstones Volume One*). Mine superintendents were beaten and murdered. The wealthy mine owners who were often affiliated with railroad companies had significant political influence during these times. In 1865 they flexed this political muscle when they persuaded the state legislature to pass a law allowing them to organize private police forces. Thus, the Coal and Iron Police were born, and the first place they appeared was in Schuylkill County. By the early 1870s, the mine owners had also hired the Pinkerton Detective Agency to infiltrate and obtain

The Battle at Little Bighorn

information on the Molly Maguires to bring their members to justice. Before the end of the decade, twenty alleged members of this group would be arrested, tried, and executed by hanging.

How is it that a Pennsylvania miner with a wife and two young children living and working in Schuylkill County in 1875 would find his way to the Little Bighorn Battlefield just a short year later. The author Genovese, based on oral family history, sets forth the proposition that Heath changed jobs during this period and became a member of the Coal and Iron Police. In 1875 the miners went on a six-month strike, and violence in the area escalated. It was alleged that the Molly Maguires would sometimes nail notices on the doors of those working to break the strike, threatening beatings and death. Again, based on family history, Genovese maintains that one morning Heath found a death notice on his front door. The author maintains that Heath responded to this notice by leaving his wife and family, promising to return when it was safe, and headed west.

According to the records of the United States Army, a William Heath from Staffordshire, England, enlisted in the service on October 9, 1875, in Cincinnati, Ohio. Heath was assigned to the Seventh Cavalry and sent to Fort Lincoln in the Dakota Territory. Here he was trained and made a company farrier. The job of the farrier was an important one as the farriers were in charge of the care of the horses. In addition to feeding and watering the mounts Heath would have been responsible for treating injured horses. After joining the Seventh, the recruit may have been expected to care for up to a hundred of the animals.

In 1876 the Seventh Cavalry was part of a campaign designed to force Indians onto their reservations. The plan called for a three-pronged pincer movement to box in the Indians. General Alfred H. Terry, under whom Custer served, moved west from Fort Lincoln. Colonel John Gibbons led his forces east from Fort Ellis, and General George Crook's expedition moved north from Fort Fetterman. On June 17, Crook's forces were defeated by Sioux warriors, but none of the other columns were aware that this had occurred.

General Terry had divided his forces sending Custer's cavalry to locate the Indian trail and follow it. Terry ordered Gibbon and his slower-moving command up the Bighorn to rendezvous at the mouth of the Little Bighorn. Both Custer and Gibbon felt they had sufficient men under their command to handle any number of Indians they might encounter. As Custer rode off, Gibbon said to him, "don't be greedy" and urged, "wait for us." Custer replied with a wave saying, "No, I will not."

On June 25, Custer reached the valley of the Little Bighorn River. His scouts advised him that an Indian village of immense size lay not far ahead. Custer believed that the Indians knew he was in the area and felt that he had to attack immediately. He broke his command into three parts. Major Marcus Reno was instructed to take the men under his command to follow the river and attack the village. Captain Frederick Benteen was sent to the left with orders to scout until he discovered Indians, an order Benteen later called "valley hunting ad infinitum." Meanwhile, Custer would move to the right and support Reno by launching his own attack on the village.

The plan, as is well known, failed miserably. Reno's forces were repulsed, and after a disorganized retreat, he and his severely shaken troops took defensive positions on what would become known as Reno Hill. He was joined there by Benteen's forces, where they were successful in repulsing Indian attacks. Meanwhile, Custer had been routed in his attack on the village, and he and every man with him had been killed. That is the story history tells, but the question asked by Genovese in his work is, did one man survive?

As noted earlier, Heath was a farrier and well acquainted with the horses. During the battle, when the troops dismounted and attempted to form a skirmish line, he may have been moving the mounts to the rear to secure them. Is it possible that seeing how the battle was progressing and knowing the strengths of the animals, Heath hopped on a healthy horse and made a successful run for it? Though it certainly seems possible that more than one of the soldiers may have seen this as a last hope for survival, Genovese rejects this view even though he contends Heath had left Pennsylvania based on threatened violence. He believes the soldiers, including Heath, would have seen their best chance of living was staying together.

Thus, Genovese sees Heath fighting to the end as his comrades fell around him. The author contends that Heath joined the last thirty or forty men alive who made a run for the river in hopes of staying alive. Indian accounts support that a group of soldiers made such a dash but, according to these Indians, the bluecoats were pursued and killed. Genovese has Heath making it to the river and concealing himself there. Though chased by the Indians, he moved between land and water as he put distance between himself and the Indians until they decided to return to the village to join in the victory celebration.

Heath then hiked for several days without any provisions save what he could find on the land. By the end of this trek, Genovese believes Heath was close to death suffering from "blistered feet from walking untold miles in wet boots, second-degree sunburn from exposure, starving, dehydrated, perhaps wounded and bleeding, delirious, and growing weaker by the moment." It is at this point, again based on oral family history, that the soldier is discovered by a family of settlers in a wagon who took him aboard and saved him. The Heath family history relates that the surname of the passing saviors was Ennis, and a woman with the group named Lavina nursed Heath back to health.

The Heath story continues with his return to Girardville in 1877. According to Genovese, he now felt safe because the Molly Maguires had been broken as an organization, and Heath returned to the mines to support his family. Around the year 1880, Heath and his family moved to Tamaqua, another town in Schuylkill County. His family grew to include a daughter who was named Lavina, which, again according to oral family history, was chosen because Heath had promised the woman who had nursed him that if he ever had a daughter, he would name her after the woman who had saved his life. Heath passed away on May 2, 1891, and was laid to rest in Tamaqua's Odd Fellows Cemetery.

The question is, is there any truth to the Heath story? The tale Genovese weaves is based mainly on oral family history. He does use tax records as proof that Heath did leave the coal region and then return a few years hence. A William Heath did enlist in the army and is listed among those who perished with Custer during his last battle. The story

Billy Heath's grave

of the death notice is based on family history, and there are no employment records to prove that Heath served as a Coal and Iron Policeman. Genovese maintains that these records may have been destroyed in a fire. The authors do question that a member of the Coal and Iron Police Force would have been frightened by a threat. During the time in question, that force was the source of at least equal the violence attributed to the organization called the Molly Maguires, which may not have even existed. It is worth noting that the Molly Maguires were suspected of murdering a Tamaqua policeman named Benjamin Yost on July 6, 1875. It was the following October that Heath joined the army. Perhaps the murder of a policeman and a death threat proved enough to cause Heath to flee the area. Today Yost lies buried in the same cemetery not far from the grave of Billy Heath.

One of the reviewers of Mr. Genovese's work wrote that the story would have worked better as a piece of historical fiction rather than actual history. The fact is we will never know whether the William Heath buried in Tamaqua rode with Custer into the valley of the Little Bighorn and lived to tell the tale.

There is one member of the Seventh Cavalry who lost his life during the battle buried in Pennsylvania. Lieutenant Benjamin Hubert Hodgson served as an adjutant to the portion of the command that Custer placed under Major Reno. During Reno's retreat, Hodgson had been shot in both legs while crossing the river and had fallen from his horse. He had managed to grab the stirrup of a passing soldier who tried to tow him across the river. As the

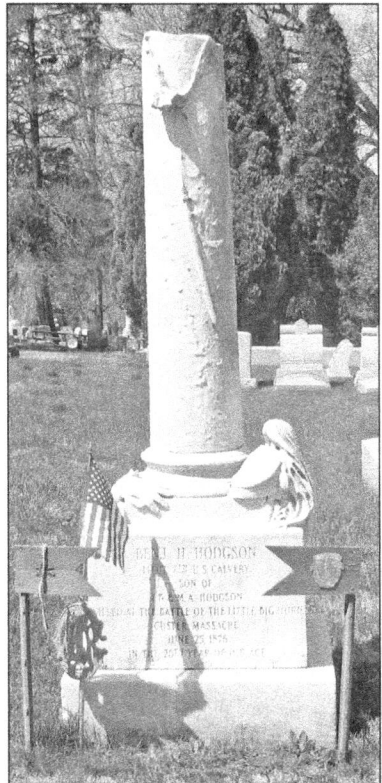

Bell Hodgson's grave

93

rider's horse lunged to make it up the riverbank, Hodgson was either shot again or passed out due to a loss of blood, and he didn't make it. His body was recovered by Sergeant Benjamin Criswell, who performed the task while under fire from the Indians. Criswell was awarded the Medal of Honor for his actions. Hodgson was initially buried on the battlefield, but his family later had his remains returned to Philadelphia, where he was reinterred at Laurel Hill Cemetery. Hodgson's watch, which was identified by its inscription, was later found in Sitting Bull's campsite. It was returned to the family.

The very mention of the Little Bighorn calls to mind one of the most famous battles in American history. The story of Custer and his men have captivated generations of Americans. The Commonwealth of Pennsylvania is undoubtedly the final resting place for one of the victims of the battle. It is also, perhaps, where the lone survivor of Custer's Last Stand was laid to rest.

13.

HENRY J. HEINZ
"The Pickle King"

County: Allegheny • Town: Pittsburgh
Buried at The Homewood Cemetery
1599 South Dallas Avenue

Henry John Heinz was the son of German immigrants who transformed his mother's recipes for horseradish and pickles into a food conglomerate that remains popular to this day. Now known mainly for his famous brand of ketchup, Heinz built his empire on his "57 Varieties" of pickles and was known as "The Pickle King" in his day.

H. J. Heinz was born on October 11, 1844, in (then) Birmingham, Pennsylvania, to John Henry Heinz (1811–1891) and Anna Margaretha Schmidt Heinz (1822–1899). Birmingham has since been incorporated into the city of Pittsburgh, comprising a portion of the Southside Flats between South 6th and South 17th Streets.

The elder Heinzes were part of the second great wave of German immigrants that occurred in the early 1800s, following the colonial-era migrations of the early to mid-1700s. They found in Pennsylvania a large population of German speakers now several generations removed from their immigrant ancestors but still maintaining their cultural preferences. Both were Lutherans who met in the Birmingham community and were married there in December 1843. Henry John was the first of eight children.

Unlike the predominantly German communities of southeastern Pennsylvania, Pittsburgh was dominated by Scotch-Irish, who ruled the upper social strata of the burgeoning iron and glass businesses. Father Heinz worked for local brickmakers to feed the construction boom occurring in the region. In the 1850s, he started his own brickyard utilizing

H. J. Heinz

the clays found along the Allegheny River. He moved the family to Sharpsburg to be closer to his business.

The Heinz family maintained a garden on their patch of land and grew vegetables, including cauliflower, carrots, potatoes, cabbage, and horseradish. Later, cucumbers and tomatoes were added. Young Heinz and his siblings would spend many hours tending the garden. By age nine, he had become an entrepreneur, selling the garden surplus to the neighbors in Sharpsburg. The following year, his parents permitted him to use nearly an acre of their land to raise the produce he thought he could sell. By age twelve, he had his own three and a half acres and upgraded his wheelbarrow to a horse and cart for making larger deliveries and to sell more product.

During his youth, Heinz experimented with different crops and seeds and meticulously recorded his observations in his journals. Heinz also studied his mother's recipes from the old country as well as the customers he met every day, learning their preferences.

During the offseason and in his spare time, Heinz did odd jobs for his neighbors, worked at his father's brickyard, and as a towpath boy on a nearby canal. At the brickyard, he learned chemistry and lessons about temperature and quality control. The canal experiences taught him about transportation.

By the time he was fifteen, Heinz had turned his focus to his produce and, most notably, horseradish, a favorite among the Germans. Making horseradish was time-consuming and was rough on the hands and eyes. Purchasing it already grated and aged provided great convenience to his customers. He bottled it in clear glass and used clear vinegar, which was rarer than brown apple cider vinegar, to highlight its purity. This soon became popular throughout the region, including hotels, restaurants, and grocers.

Over the next six years, through 1865, Heinz went to Duff's Mercantile College in Pittsburgh, where he learned accounting. He took over bookkeeping duties at the brickyard as well as his own business. During this time, he did not serve in the military during the Civil War. The Heinz family, as devout Lutherans, were anti-slavery and likely pacifists. They were also pro-Lincoln. However, draft boards often excused sons who were essential to family businesses. It appears this may have been the case with Heinz. By age twenty-one, just after the war had ended, he was a full partner with his father and continued to build his produce and horseradish business.

In 1869, Heinz partnered with his friends, L. Clarence and E. J. Noble, to start Heinz Noble & Company involved in the marketing of packaged horseradish, fruit preserves, mustard, pickles, and catsup. They sold to hotels, restaurants, and grocers in the Pittsburgh area and soon expanded to neighboring cities, eventually reaching into Ohio and the East Coast.

Also, in 1869, Heinz married an Irish girl named Sarah "Sallie" Sloan Young, a Presbyterian. The two had a daughter, Irene, in 1871, and a son, Clarence Noble Heinz, in 1873. Sons Howard, 1877; Robert, 1882; and Clifford, 1883, soon followed, though Robert died in infancy. All the children were raised as Presbyterians, and Heinz migrated away from the Lutheran Church.

As the young family grew, so did Heinz Noble & Company. They added sauerkraut and vinegar to the mix and sold their products under brand labels and in individual packaging rather than as commodities in nondescript barrels. At its peak, the company employed 150 people turning out 500 barrels of sauerkraut, 15,000 barrels of pickles, and 50,000 barrels of vinegar. Then came the depression of 1873. As Jay Cooke's bank failed in Philadelphia and the railroad boom went bust, the economy in the United States, like most economies in the western world, collapsed. Times became very hard, and suddenly Heinz and his partners were in trouble. In 1875, the company went bankrupt, and Heinz slipped into a deep personal depression.

During the centennial year of 1876, Heinz had renewed energy and was back on his feet. The family pooled together $3,000 and formed F&J Heinz Company. Heinz's wife, Sarah, owned half of the company while mother, Anna; brother, John; and cousin, Frederick each had one-sixth.

Over the next five years, Heinz repaid all the debts incurred by Heinz Noble & Company. Sales rocketed from $99,000 in 1879 to $381,000 by 1884. By 1888, he consolidated the family holdings under himself and renamed the company H. J. Heinz, at which point sales topped $1.2 million. Sales doubled again by 1896, at which point he had 18,000 seasonal and 2,000 year-round employees.

By the turn of the century, H. J. Heinz Company had offices in New York, Philadelphia, Chicago, St. Paul, Cincinnati, Denver, San Francisco, London, and several other cities. Factories were built close to fields, and more foreign agencies were added around the globe. Having learned harsh lessons from his prior failure, Heinz built the business using internal cash flow. This insulated the company from the economic recessions in 1893 and 1907.

In 1896, Heinz introduced the slogan "57 varieties," referring to the more than sixty different products they were selling. Five and seven were his and his wife's lucky numbers. He was inspired by an advertisement he had seen in New York for a shoe store boasting "21 different styles." His was now the largest food company in the United States and likely the world. Though Campbell's in soup, French's in mustard, and Van

Early Heinz train advertising

Camp's in beans were strong in narrow categories, Heinz was successful more broadly and on a larger scale. He was also a master of marketing and advertising, utilizing billboards and brightly painted wagons with his logos. He also created unique bottle shapes to package his products, especially his world-famous tomato ketchup.

In 1905, H. J. Heinz Company incorporated, and Heinz was the first president, holding this position for the rest of his life. By 1910, the company hit $6 million in sales and employed more than 40,000 seasonal and 4,000 permanent workers and was known for the generous treatment of his employees. He had also become an expert proponent of food safety.

As he became more successful, Heinz delegated more and more of the operation to his son, Howard, and his brother-in-law, Sebastian Mueller. He then became involved in philanthropic and civic activities, hobbies, and international travel. Heinz remained committed to the Pittsburgh area, building his mansion, Greenlawn, there while other Pittsburghers like Andrew Carnegie moved to New York or Europe.

Heinz turned 74 on October 11, 1918, just as the Spanish flu was raging around the world. Seven months later, at approximately 3:50 P.M. on Wednesday, May 14, 1919, Heinz succumbed to pneumonia at Greenlawn. That Friday, after a short service at the mansion, Heinz's casket was taken to the East Liberty Presbyterian Church, where it lay in state for nearly three hours while many paid their respects. He was then

The Heinz family crypt

interred at Homewood Cemetery in the mausoleum constructed after his wife, Sallie's, death from typhoid in 1894.

Heinz left significant gifts to the University of Pittsburgh, which led to the building of the Heinz Chapel there. His son Howard took over the company until he died in 1941. Heinz's grandson, H. J. "Jack" Heinz II, led the company until 1966. He was the last family member to lead the company.

Heinz's great-grandson, H. J. "John" Heinz III, became a United States Senator for Pennsylvania who was killed in a plane crash in 1991. The senator's widow, Teresa Heinz, subsequently married Senator John Kerry, who later became a presidential candidate and secretary of state.

Heinz also was a second cousin to Frederick Trump, the grandfather of Donald Trump of New York, the President of the United States.

Today, the H. J. Heinz company is part of the Kraft Heinz Company, partially owned by Warren Buffet's Berkshire Hathaway. Heinz Ketchup remains the number one ketchup brand in the United States and boasts 150 number one or number two brands worldwide.

14.

BETTY MATTAS JAMES

"Everyone Knows It's Slinky"

County: Blair • Town: Altoona
Buried at Alto-Reste Burial Park
109 Alto-Reste Park

This woman came up with the name for one of the world's best-known toys. Though it was invented by her husband, she was a partner in the business that initially built and marketed his unique invention. In 1960 her husband left the firm and his family, and she was put in the position of not only raising her six children but running and managing the business on her own. Under her leadership, the company flourished. She did so well that in 2001 she was inducted into the Toy Industry Hall of Fame. Her name was Betty Mattas James, and the toy she named was the Slinky.

Betty Mattas was born on February 13, 1918, in Altoona, Pennsylvania. She was the only child of Clair and Irene Mattas. After graduating from Altoona High School, Betty attended Pennsylvania State University. It was here she met her future husband, Richard James. The pair were wed in 1940 just one year before the Japanese attack on Pearl Harbor drew the United States into World War II.

Richard James studied mechanical engineering at Penn State and graduated in 1939. He was working at William Cramp & Sons Shipbuilding Company, located in Philadelphia, when the country entered the war. The company had a contract with the United States government. As part of the war effort, its employees built submarines and tugboats. As an engineer, James addressed problems that ships on the high seas were

Betty James

encountering at the time. It was while he was working on the challenge of rough seas damaging nautical instruments that a fortunate miscue led to his invention of the Slinky. While attacking the problem, James inadvertently knocked a spring off his work area and then watched it as it made what looked like a few steps across the room. James had grown up during the Great Depression and, as a youngster, had built many of his own toys. Watching the spring, he may have thought back to those days. What we do know is that when he got home, he told Betty what had happened and said he believed he could make an inexpensive toy that kids could have fun with.

James worked and perfected his invention, but it was his wife who took on the chore of naming the new toy. Betty went page by page through a dictionary for two days before deciding she had found the appropriate name. She settled on the word "slinky," an adjective that means graceful and sinuous in movement, line, or figure. She thought it captured the toy's essence, and her husband agreed.

Now, of course, the couple had to figure out how to market the toy. They created a company and named it the James Spring and Wire Company. Then they borrowed the money necessary to make hundreds of Slinkys. They took the toy to multiple retailers without success. The view of many of these store owners was that the Slinky wasn't all that exciting. Finally, the Gimbels Store in Philadelphia gave them a shot. They were given one end of a counter which they could use to demonstrate the toy. Betty was so apprehensive about the possible sales that day that she gave a friend a dollar to buy the product, hoping to spur other sales. It turns out she could have kept the dollar as the entire stock of 400 sold out at one dollar apiece. By Christmas Day 1945, approximately 22,000 Slinkys had been sold.

The business prospered, and by 1956 the couple had renamed their enterprise James Industries. By now, the family had grown to six children. They were all living in a beautiful home in the Philadelphia suburbs. It is possible that Richard was never comfortable with success. In 1988 Betty described her husband as "a dreamer." In 1960 Richard told Betty he was moving to Bolivia to join a religious group to whom he had been donating large amounts of money. He wanted Betty and the children to go with him. Betty wouldn't think of uprooting her children, who were quite happy where they were. Richard left on his own, leaving Betty the business to run and their children to raise. The couple divorced in 1961, and Richard passed away in Bolivia in 1974.

As a result of Richard's religious donations, Betty was left with a business operating in debt. She moved the company's manufacturing plant from the Philadelphia area to Hollidaysburg, Pennsylvania, where she had family available to help care for her children. Betty also planned to pay back the company's creditors. By the time she was finished, she had paid off hundreds of thousands in loans and sent these creditors personally written thank you notes. Under her guidance, the company flourished.

In Betty's view, she had an ideal toy. She described it as not only being simple but as ". . . a universal toy. It's a toy that doesn't need any explanation. It has intrinsic play value. There are very few other toys like that." Her attitude and enthusiasm may well have saved the company. Although even during down periods she was reluctant to raise prices. Robert Lestochi remembers that when the company was going through a hard time in the 1970s it took some convincing to get her to approve a wholesale price increase from $5.40 to $5.80 for a dozen Slinkys. She was determined to keep the toy affordable for all families.

In 1962 Betty demonstrated her business savvy when she decided to advertise the Slinky on television. She had seen how people had purchased the toy after seeing it in action. She hired musicians to write a jingle for the commercials. Homer Fesperman and Charles Weagley composed what Tim Walsh called in *The Playmakers: Amazing Origins of Timeless Toys*, the longest-running jingle in advertising history. There are still many alive today who could sing the jingle word for word.

Betty ran the company for 38 years. Under her direction, several new Slinky products were produced, including the Slinky Train and the Slinky Dog. In 1995 Walt Disney Pictures used the Slinky Dog as a character in the movie *Toy Story*. Betty had her Slinky Dog changed to match the one in the film. It proved to be another wise move. In the initial year after the movie was released, the demand for the toy soared.

By this time, Betty had turned the spring company into a multimillion-dollar business. She was getting multiple offers from others who wanted to buy the business. To her credit, she was loyal to her family, her employees, and, most of all, to her customers. She stayed in charge of the company until she was eighty years old when she sold the company under the condition that the Slinky factory would remain in Hollidaysburg.

The Slinky has been used in several ways. Teachers at both the high school and college level have used Slinkys to simulate the properties of waves. NASA has used the toy aboard the space shuttle in zero-gravity experiments. It's even been used in music. In 1959 John Cage composed a work called *Sounds of Venice* that used among the instruments an amplified Slinky. One can also go online and view videos where the toy has been used to keep squirrels from accessing bird feeders.

In 1999, the United States Postal Service issued a Slinky postage stamp. A year later the Slinky was inducted into the National Toy Hall of Fame. In 2001 Betty James was inducted into the Toy Industry Association's Hall of Fame. Two years later the Slinky was named to the Century of Toys List, which detailed the 100 most memorable and creative toys of the 20th century.

In 2001 a bill to make the Slinky the Pennsylvania State Toy was introduced but failed to be enacted. Bob Swain, a Pennsylvanian from Bucks County, has carried on the work attempting to get the state legislature to pass such a bill. Swain notes that Pennsylvania has a state dog, a state flower, a state insect, and a state beverage. He sees no reason why a state toy can't come into being, and he views the Slinky as a natural to fill that position.

Betty James died at the age of 90 in Philadelphia of congestive heart failure. She was laid to rest in the Alto Reste Burial Park located in Altoona, Pennsylvania. She was a remarkable businesswoman who was undoubtedly ahead of her time. Without her, generations of boys and girls may never have gotten to know the Slinky.

The grave of Betty James

15.

FLORENCE FOSTER JENKINS
"The Glory (????) of the Human Voice"

County: Luzerne • Town: Wilkes-Barre
Buried at Hollenback Cemetery
504 North River Street

Many said she had an unforgettable voice. One reporter described it as coming around but once in a generation, though he followed that observation
by saying that was the public's good fortune. She was born into a wealthy
Pennsylvania family and was well educated in the arts. She had a talent for
the piano, but after an arm injury limited her options with that instrument, she decided she wanted to sing opera. The problem was her talent in
this area was notably lacking. In his book documenting the world's heroic
failures, Stephen Pile called her "the world's worst opera singer" writing
that, "no one, before or since, has succeeded in liberating themselves quite
so completely from the shackles of musical notation." This is not to say she
has not had her admirers. In 1968 she was one of two singers mentioned
by Barbara Streisand, who was responding to a query asking which other
singers she would like to be. The other singer mentioned by Streisand was
Ray Charles. In 2003 David Bowie cited the RCA album of her recordings
as one of his most significant discoveries. She lived most of her adult life
in New York City, and her crowning achievement came in 1944 when she
performed in that city's Carnegie Hall. Lacking rhythm and pitch did not
stand in the way of her becoming one of America's most famous sopranos.
Her name was Florence Foster Jenkins.

Jenkins was born on July 19, 1868, in Wilkes-Barre, Pennsylvania.
Her mother was Mary Jane Hoagland Foster, and her father, Charles

Florence Foster Jenkins

Dorrance Foster, was a successful attorney and a descendant of wealthy Pennsylvania landowners. The couple had only one other child, another daughter named Lillian, who contracted diphtheria and passed away at the age of eight in 1883.

As a girl, Jenkins developed a fondness for the piano, and her parents supported her interest in the instrument. She would later claim to have begun performing as a soloist at the age of ten, though other reports have her performing at society functions as "Little Miss Foster" when she was just seven years old. It is also possible that she performed for President

Rutherford B. Hayes when he visited Wilkes-Barre on July 3, 1878, where he was the principal speaker at the centennial commemoration of the Battle of Wyoming. In 2016 local Wilkes Barre historian, Anthony Brooks, said it was "absolutely plausible" that Jenkins met the president because her father served on the board of the Wyoming Commemorative Association.

At the age of ten, Jenkins was enrolled in a boarding school, the Moravian Seminary, located in Bethlehem, Pennsylvania. Though most of the students were Pennsylvania natives, those enrolled at Moravian included young women from all parts of the United States, as well as from Canada, England, and South American countries. The course of study leaned heavily on religion, and according to two of Jenkins biographers, Nicholas Martin and Jasper Rees, the goal of the institution was to produce "young women with an instinct for good behavior." Moravian did offer plenty of opportunities for her to continue with the piano as there were 46 of them on campus.

No one is certain when she met her husband, Dr. Frank Thornton Jenkins. He did have a sister, who also attended Moravian, so it is possible that their paths crossed when he was visiting. What we do know is that on June 29, 1883, Lillian Foster died, and ten days after the burial of her sister, the then 14-year old Jenkins eloped and married a man sixteen years her senior. The couple settled in Philadelphia. She left her husband after a year upon learning that he had infected her with syphilis. She would later claim to have been granted a divorce in 1902, but no documentation supporting this has ever been found. Though she never spoke to Dr. Jenkins again, she retained the surname for the rest of her life.

In 1886 Jenkins enrolled in a two-year course at the Philadelphia Academy of Music. Based on a report that appeared in an 1888 edition of the *Wilkes-Barre Record,* she appears to have done well at the academy. The paper reported that she was currently ranked second in a class of over 800. It described her as "a brilliant musician and is so considered in classical circles." After an arm injury ended any hopes Jenkins had of being a concert pianist, she gave piano lessons to support herself.

In 1909 her father died, and his will made Jenkins the beneficiary of a sizable trust. She and her mother moved to New York City, where she decided to pursue a musical career as a singer. She began taking singing lessons and joined multiple social clubs whose members were other wealthy New Yorkers. She began producing *tableaux vivants,* which were popular among the well-off in society at the time. Jenkins designed her elaborate costumes for her appearances at these events.

That first year in New York also brought another man into her life. Jenkins was forty years of age when she met a thirty-three-year-old English actor named St. Clair Bayfield. Years later, she recalled seeing Bayfield for the first time. "Why there is a man with the loveliest smile which I have ever seen in my life." She and Bayfield began a common-law relationship that would last the rest of her life.

Jenkins started singing at small musical events for her friends. She also performed on an annual basis in some larger venues like the Ritz Carlton ballroom. For these appearances, she refused to sell tickets to news reporters or critics, preferring an audience that consisted of friends and admirers. She soon became a musical cult figure in New York City, beginning in the roaring twenties and lasting until her death in 1944. She counted Cole Porter and Lily Pons among her fans. Porter rarely missed one of her recitals, but it was reported that he would bang his cane into his foot so he would not break out laughing when she sang. The poet Walter Meredith described her recitals as "never exactly an aesthetic experience, or only to the degree that an early Christian among the lions provided an aesthetic experience; it was chiefly immolatory, and Madame Jenkins was always eaten, in the end." The opera impresario Ira Siff said, "Jenkins was exquisitely bad, so bad that it added up to quite a good evening of theater."

In the early forties, Jenkins entered the Melotone Recording Studio in New York and, at her own expense, recorded nine selections on five 78 RPM records. She sold these to friends for $2.50. In the recordings, she was joined by her pianist, Cosme McMoon, who can be heard adjusting to her rhythm errors and consistent tempo variations. Still, there was little he could do about her delivering the numbers in a consistently flat manner. Seven of the selections were released by RCA Victor in 1954 and again in 1962 on a twelve-inch LP titled *The Glory (????) of the Human Voice.* This is the record David Bowie listed as one of his great discoveries. Sony Classical released a compact disc version in 1992.

At the age of 76, on October 25, 1944, prodded by public demand, Jenkins performed before a general admission audience at Carnegie Hall. A recreation of this concert was later featured in the movie *Florence Foster Jenkins* starring Meryl Streep in the title role. The film premiered in London and New York City in 2016. Streep received critical acclaim for her performance and an Academy Award nomination.

Tickets to the 2,800-seat venue sold out weeks in advance, and as many as 2,000 people were turned away at the door on the evening of the recital. Those who were able to gain entrance included Cole Porter (who certainly brought his cane); the renowned soprano Lily Pons (who was escorted by her husband the orchestra conductor, Andre Kostelanetz; burlesque star Gypsy Rose Lee; Kitty Carlisle; and the dance model for several Disney characters including Snow White, Marge Champion. Because Jenkins had no control over the sale of tickets, the audience also included multiple music critics and reporters.

When she appeared on the stage, she was greeted with a tremendous ovation that went on for several minutes. What followed was, in all probability, one of the most unusual shows in the hallowed hall's history. Marge Champion recalled, "I was just totally unprepared for the fact that it did not seem to bother her in the least that everyone in the audience was convulsed in laughter nor was she in any other way thrilled by it. I don't know what she did with it. I don't know how she processed that laughter."

A critic commented, "Her notes range from the impossible to the fantastic and bear no relationship whatsoever to any known score or scale."

McMoon sitting at his piano, remembered it as the noisiest audience he had ever performed before. When she delivered the song "Clavelitos," during which she tossed rosebuds at the audience, McMoon reported that one well-known actress was carried out of her box in a state of hysteria.

When he was leaving the concert, Earl Wilson of the *New York Post* ran into her common-law husband and asked, "Why?"

Bayfield replied, "She loves music."

Wilson responded, "If she loves music, why does she do this?"

The critics were not kind. Richard S. Davis wrote, "Mme. Jenkins, if you haven't heard, and the chances are you haven't, is a lady who gives

The grave of Florence Foster Jenkins

song recitals because there is no law against it. Mme. Jenkins bills herself as a coloratura soprano, which means that she takes the songs that bring out the best in Lily Pons and permits them to bring out her worst. And the worst of Mme. Jenkins, you are herewith assured, is something awful."

Whether she was bothered by the negative press, we will never know. She knew she had her detractors as years before Carnegie Hall she remarked to a friend, "People may say I can't sing, but no one can ever say I didn't sing."

Five days after the concert, Jenkins was shopping when she suffered a heart attack. She died one month later, on November 26, 1944, in her Manhattan residence. Her remains were returned to the city of her birth, and she was laid to rest in the Foster family mausoleum in Wilkes-Barre's Hollenback Cemetery.

16.

JAMES W. McCORD, JR.

"A White House Plumber"

County: Lebanon • Town: Annville
Buried at Indiantown Gap National Cemetery
RR#2 Indiantown Gap Road

He served the United States as a bombardier during World War II. After the war, he attended the University of Texas, and in 1949 he graduated from that institution with a degree in business administration. He served as an FBI special agent before joining the CIA in 1951. In 1972 shortly after he resigned his position with the CIA, he was hired by President Nixon's re-election committee. He was among five men arrested during a break-in at the Watergate complex offices of the Democratic National Committee. After being convicted and receiving a sentence of 25 years in federal prison, he sent a letter to the judge that implicated senior officials in the Nixon administration of covering up a conspiracy that led to the break-in. This letter and his decision to become a cooperating witness have been pointed to as the event that broke the Watergate case "wide open." His name was James W. McCord, Jr.

McCord was born in Waurika, Oklahoma, on January 26, 1924. In the book *All the President's Men*, authors Carl Bernstein and Bob Woodward write about compiling background information on McCord after his arrest at the Watergate complex. Through a telephone book, they found the number for the private security consulting agency that McCord was running at the time. Their phone calls to the business went unanswered. However, the business address showed that it was in a large office building with many other tenants. The two reporters divided the

James McCord, Jr.

names of the tenets and began calling them. An attorney who had offices in the building recalled the name of a girl who had worked for McCord in the summer months. That information led to contact with the girl's father, who said he knew McCord and provided information on him as well as the names of other friends Woodward might want to contact.

Based on these efforts that resulted in multiple contacts with those who knew or had done business with McCord, Woodward put together a profile of the man apprehended in the Watergate complex. It read, "A native of the Texas Panhandle; deeply religious, active in the First Baptist Church of Washington; father of an Air Force Academy cadet and a retarded daughter; ex-FBI agent; military reservist; former chief of physical security for the CIA; teacher of a security course at Montgomery Junior College; a family man; extremely conscientious; quiet; reliable." Though Nixon's Attorney General had denied that McCord worked on the re-election committee, McCord's friends were telling Woodward that he was working on the committee full time. Others referred to McCord's "rocklike" character and described him as the consummate "government man" who had total respect for the chain of command and would follow orders without question.

McCord was indeed a government man. He had spent his adult life in the service of his country—first in the armed forces followed by stints in the FBI and CIA. When he was at the CIA, the then director of the agency, Allen Dulles, introduced McCord to an Air Force colonel as "the best man we have."

In 1961, under McCord's direction, the CIA began a counterintelligence program aimed against the Fair Play for Cuba Committee (FPCC). McCord's work directing this program would undoubtedly have put him in touch with other agency employees who would later join him in the Watergate saga. These included E. Howard Hunt and Frank Sturgis. Indeed, McCord would also surely have been aware of the activities of Lee Harvey Oswald when the alleged presidential assassin set up his own one-man branch of the FPCC in New Orleans. McCord's work in this area would have also brought him into contact with David Atlee Phillips. Phillips was a CIA agent who was active in running an anti-Castro media campaign in New Orleans. There are several reports of at least one actual meeting between Oswald and Phillips. In August of 1963, Oswald was arrested in a scene that received widespread TV coverage in the New Orleans area. He was seen handing out flyers on behalf of the FPCC. He was then confronted and got into a fight with a member of the anti-Castro *Directorio Revolucionario Estudiantil* (DRE) (English translation: Student Revolutionary Directorate).

Days before the fight, Oswald wrote to the New York office of the FPCC and described the incident which had yet to occur. The head of the DRE at the time was David Phillips. There are many conspiracy

McCord testifying at the Watergate hearings

theories regarding the JFK assassination and the involvement of the CIA. Phillips, Hunt, and Sturgis all play prominent roles in these conspiracy theories. Shane O'Sullivan, in his book *Dirty Tricks,* quotes Alfred Baldwin, a former FBI agent, as claiming that McCord was in Dallas the day of the assassination. The same allegation has been made relative to Phillips, Hunt, and Sturgis.

After Hunt died, his sons, Howard St. John Hunt and David Hunt, went public with claims that their father made recordings that contained revelations relating to himself and others being involved in the JFK assassination. The sons claim that his father implicated CIA officials, including Cord Meyer, the ex-husband of Mary Pinchot Meyer (See *Keystone Tombstones Volume Three*), Phillips, Sturgis, and William Harvey. McCord was not mentioned. The *Los Angeles Times* reviewed the information provided by the Hunt sons to support their story and found it "inconclusive." Some in the Hunt family viewed the sons' efforts as an attempt to cash in on their father's death.

In 1971 McCord left the CIA to work for the Nixon administration on the Committee for the Re-election of the President, which was commonly known as CREEP. It is unclear why McCord decided to leave the agency as it appeared he was held in high regard by the then director Richard Helms. Initially, his job involved gathering derogatory information on Nixon's perceived enemies. Following that, he joined what was called "the plumbers unit," named for the role of this unit in plugging information leaks.

On the evening of June 17, 1972, McCord led a team of "plumbers," that included Sturgis and three Cuban exiles, into the offices of the Democratic National Committee in the Watergate building. Their purpose was to inspect malfunctioning bugging devices that they had installed there during a previous break-in. A security guard observed a taped-over door latch and notified the police. The authorities arrived and arrested the five men. Hunt and G. Gordon Liddy, who oversaw the planning of the operation and were coordinating the activities of the five burglars from an adjacent building, fled the scene but were later arrested as well. When McCord was before the judge during his arraignment, he was questioned about his employment. His whispered answer "CIA" got the attention of *Washington Post* reporter Bob Woodward.

The last residence of James McCord in Douglassville

McCord was one of the first men convicted in the Watergate saga. U.S. District Judge John Sirica sentenced him to 25 years in federal prison. McCord then wrote a letter to Sirica saying that some of his testimony had been perjured because of pressure from the White House Counsel, John Dean, and the former Attorney General, John Mitchell. In the letter, McCord requested a meeting with the judge and stated, "Several members of my family have expressed concern for my life if I disclose knowledge of the facts in this matter . . . In the interests of justice . . . of restoring faith in the criminal justice system." He said he was coming forward to tell the truth. McCord then became a cooperating witness, and that cooperation eventually led to impeachment proceedings and the resignation of President Richard Nixon.

Based on his cooperation, McCord's sentence was reduced to four months. He made a statement as he was entering the federal prison in Allenwood, Pennsylvania, that, "In the long run it has been extremely beneficial to the country to become aware of what occurred." However, what took place has been the subject of debate for decades. Some researchers believe that McCord may have been part of a plan to get caught and implicate White House officials. They point to the amateur taping of the door latches and the fact that incriminating evidence was left in the Watergate hotel room where Hunt and Liddy monitored the situation as evidence of a set-up. These researchers find it difficult to believe that someone with McCord's experience would have been part of such a clumsy operation.

It has been pointed out that without McCord's letter and his testimony, the Nixon administration may have been successful in stonewalling the investigation. Some believe that McCord spoke out to protect the

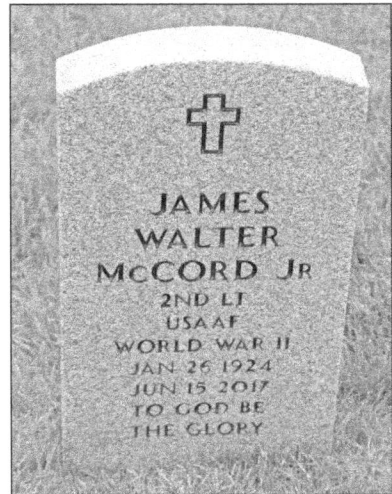

McCord's grave

CIA—that is, to keep investigators focused on the White House involvement. Author Jim Hougan in his work on Watergate, *Secret Agenda*, points out that in McCord's CREEP Office, he hung a picture of former CIA Director Richard Helms rather than one of President Nixon. The photo was inscribed, "To Jim, with deep appreciation," and the word deep was underlined. The CIA has often been implicated in the assassination of JFK; might they also have decided that Nixon's efforts to improve relations with China and Russia warranted his removal?

After serving his brief prison term, McCord established his own security firm before retiring to Pennsylvania. He passed away from cancer on June 15, 2017, in Douglassville. The news media did not report his death until November 2019. He was laid to rest in Indiantown Gap National Cemetery.

I7.

MARGARET MEAD

"An American Pioneer"

County: Bucks • Town: Buckingham
Buried at Trinity Buckingham Church
2631 Durham Road

When Margaret Mead died in 1978, she was the most famous anthropologist in the world. It was through her work that many people learned about anthropology, which is the study of human beings and their origin, distribution, and relationships. She endures as the world's best known and most influential cultural anthropologist who not only popularized anthropology, but some say laid the foundation for the sexual revolution of the 1960s, through her reports detailing the attitudes toward sex in South Pacific and Southeast Asian cultures.

Mead was the oldest of five children born to Edward Mead, a professor of finance at the University of Pennsylvania and Emily Fogg Mead, a sociologist who studied Italian immigrants. She was born on December 16, 1901, in Philadelphia but raised in nearby Doylestown. She grew up in a free-thinking intellectual home, and her grandmother, Martha Ramsay Mead, played an active role in her life. Martha Mead was a child psychologist and taught Mead to watch the behavior of the younger children to figure out the reasons behind their actions. Her family had a variety of religious outlooks, and Mead chose the Episcopal Church at age 11 and remained a member throughout her life.

Mead entered DePauw University in 1919 and transferred to Barnard College in New York a year later, where she majored in Psychology. Her senior year anthropology course taught by famous anthropologist Franz

Margaret Mead

Boas was an important event in her life since it was then she decided to become an anthropologist. She graduated from Barnard in 1923 and entered graduate school at Columbia. That same year she married Luther Cressman. At that time, the Anthropology Department at Columbia consisted of Boas and Ruth Benedict, who would become a lifelong friend and lover. Mead was granted a master's degree from Columbia in 1924 and a Ph.D. in 1929.

In 1925 she set out for American Samoa, where she did her first field-work, focusing on adolescent girls. During this field trip, she gathered material for the first of her 23 books, *Coming of Age in Samoa*, a perennial bestseller. The book established her reliance on observation rather than sta-tistics for data. This was controversial and remains a bone of contention to this day. The book generated a great deal of coverage both in the academic world and in the popular press. At the time the book was published, the idea of living with native people was groundbreaking. The book upset many westerners who felt shocked by her observation that young Samoan women deferred marriage for many years while enjoying casual sex before eventually choosing a husband. As a landmark study regarding sexual mores, the book frequently came under attack on ideological grounds. The National Catholic Register and the conservative Intercollegiate Studies Institute were both extremely critical. The Intercollegiate Studies Institute listed it number 1 on its list of the 50 Worst Books of the Twentieth Century. Mead's research methodology also came in for criticism from fellow anthropologists and reviewers for making sweeping generalizations based on a relatively short period of study.

On her return to the U.S., she began her long association with the American Museum of Natural History in New York City. In 1928 she divorced Luther Cressman and married Reo Fortune, an anthropologist from New Zealand. Fortune accompanied Mead in 1928 when she went to New Guinea to study the thought of young children. This study of children's thinking in its sociological context is described in *Growing Up in New Guinea*. She compares their views on family, marriage, sex, child-rearing, and religion to those of Westerners.

Mead's marriage to Fortune ended in divorce, and in 1936 she married Gregory Bateson, a British anthropologist. They had a daughter Mary Catherine Bateson who would also become an anthropologist. The couple's pediatrician was the famous Benjamin Spock who incorporated some of Mead's practices and beliefs acquired from her fieldwork. Breastfeeding on demand rather than on a schedule was one.

Mead readily admitted that Bateson was the husband she loved the most and was devastated when he left her in 1950. She remained his loving friend ever after, keeping his photo by her bedside wherever she traveled, including beside her hospital deathbed.

In 1936 Mead and Bateson headed together for fieldwork in Bali, which is in Indonesia. They lived there to explore the role of culture in personality formation. The study was especially noteworthy for the development of new field techniques, most notably the extensive use of film and still photographs. These made it possible to record and analyze important details that had escaped the pencil and paper notes. The publication of *Balinese Character* in 1942 marks a change in the recording and presentation of ethnological data and may be one of her most significant contributions to the science of anthropology.

When World War II cut off field research in the South Pacific, Mead and Ruth Benedict pioneered the application of anthropological techniques to the study of contemporary cultures, founding the Institute for Intercultural Studies. Mead also served on the National Research Council's Committee on Food Habits. From 1946 to 1969, she served as curator of ethnology at the American Museum of Natural History and was elected a Fellow of the American Academy of Arts and Sciences in 1948.

Mead taught at The New School and at Columbia University, where she was an adjunct professor from 1954 to 1978. She was a professor of anthropology and chair of the Division of Social Science at Fordham University's Lincoln Center campus from 1968 to 1970, founding their anthropology department. In 1970 she joined the faculty of the University of Rhode Island. In 1976 she was inducted into the National Women's Hall of Fame.

Mead spent her last years in a close relationship with anthropologist Rhoda Metraux with whom she lived from 1955 onward. Published letters between the two establish a romantic relationship.

Margaret Mead died in New York City on November 15, 1978, and was buried in Trinity Episcopal Church Cemetery in Buckingham, Pennsylvania. On January 19, 1979, President Jimmy Carter announced that he was awarding the Presidential Medal of Freedom posthumously to Mead. United Nations Ambassador Andrew Young presented the award to Mead's daughter.

There is no question that Mead was one of the leading American intellectuals of the twentieth century. She authored some twenty books and coauthored an equal number. She was much honored in her lifetime, serving as president of major scientific associations, including the

American Anthropological Association and the American Association for the Advancement of Science. She also received twenty-eight honorary doctorates.

Through her best-selling books, her lectures, and her well-read column in *Redbook* magazine, Mead popularized anthropology in the United States. She was also a role model for American women, encouraging them to pursue professional careers previously closed to women while at the same time championing their roles as mothers. She believed that cultural patterns of racism, warfare, and environmental exploitation were learned and that members of a society could work together to modify their traditions and construct new institutions.

Margaret Mead's grave

18.

HERBERT MORRISON

"Oh, the Humanity!"

County: Westmorland • Town: Scottdale
Buried at Scottdale Cemetery
1108 South Broadway Street

On May 6, 1937, the pride of Nazi Germany, the airship christened the *Hindenburg* prepared for a routine landing at an airfield located in Lakehurst, New Jersey. The ship was considered the luxury liner of the air. It had been constructed to make the travelers on board as comfortable as possible. On this trip to the United States, the *Hindenburg* carried half its full capacity of passengers, 36 of a possible 70. The ship was fully booked for its return flight. The ship was manned by 61 crew members. Watching from below was a thirty-one-year-old radio journalist who had been assigned to cover the ship's arrival for a delayed broadcast. As the airship was attempting to dock with its mooring mast, the *Hindenburg* burst into flames. The dramatic recorded report of the disaster delivered by the journalist was later added to a film of the ship's destruction. It became one of the most famous and viewed newsreels in history. That journalist's name was Herbert Morrison.

Morrison was born on May 14, 1905, in Connellsville, Pennsylvania. Little is known about his early life. He graduated from Scottdale High School in 1923, and it appears he wanted to go to West Point. The July 24, 1923, edition of the *Pittsburgh Press* carried a small story about a Scottdale youth identified as Herbert Oglevee Morrison who had been nominated by Congressman Clyde Kelly for admission to the academy. For whatever reason, Morrison never attended West Point and instead headed to Chicago, where he became a reporter for the radio station WLS.

Morrison developed an interest in flying and became a pilot in 1929. When flooding occurred in the Ohio and Mississippi valleys in 1937, Morrison covered the events by air. It was during this period that he came to know several officials who worked for American Airlines. It was the airline which offered Morrison one of their planes so he could fly to Lakehurst, New Jersey, to cover the *Hindenburg*'s initial arrival of the 1937 season. The management at WLS had refused to send Morrison to report on the airship's arrival, but when they learned that the airline was going to pay for the trip, they gave the okay. Morrison

Herbert Morrison

also argued that the event would allow him and his sound engineer, Charles Nehlsen, to test out some new recording equipment. What seems apparent is this was an assignment Morrison was determined to land.

As Morrison and Nehlsen watched the *Hindenburg* approach the airfield, they saw the largest object ever to fly. The ship would make the 747 airliners that carry us today look small by comparison. It was more than three times larger than the biggest passenger jets that take to our skies. The *Hindenburg* could cross the Atlantic in fewer than three days, and at the time, it was the fastest means of going from one continent to another. The average trip by sea took twice as long. It also offered comfort and luxury with a smoking and a dining room. Passengers traveled in twenty-five cabins but could also spend their time in the lounge, which offered an observation deck to enjoy the sights below. One of our modern-day blimps could easily be hidden behind a *Hindenburg* tail fin. However, today blimps are filled with non-flammable helium gas, while *Hindenburg's* gas bags were filled with flammable hydrogen gas. The great ship carried seven million cubic feet of it.

Morrison began his coverage by offering a plug to the airline that had delivered him from Chicago. He noted that he and Nehlsen and flown from Chicago to New York nonstop aboard a new 21-passenger American Airlines plane. He added that the trip had only taken 3 hours and 55 minutes. He concluded this ringing endorsement by adding, "And incidentally, American Airlines is the only airline in the United States which makes connections with the *Hindenburg*."

A light rain had begun to fall as the giant airship dropped its mooring lines from an altitude of about 295 feet. Four minutes later, some of the witnesses reported seeing fabric ahead of the upper fin flutter, and others said they saw a dim blue flame. Passengers heard a detonation, and some in the front of the *Hindenburg* felt a shock which officers would later say they thought had been caused by a broken rope. The ship caught fire and was soon engulfed in flames.

Reporting from below, Morrison described the scene, "It's practically standing still now they've dropped ropes out of the nose of the ship; and (uh) they've been taken ahold of down on the field by a number of men. It's starting to rain again; it's . . . the rain had (uh) slacked up a little bit. The back motors of the ship are just holding it (uh) just enough to keep it from . . . It's burst into flames! It's burst into flames, and it's falling, it's crashing! It's crashing terrible! Watch it, watch it, folks! Get out of the way, get out of the way! Get this, Charlie; get this, Charlie! It's fire . . . and it's crashing! It's crashing terrible! Oh my! Get out of the way, please! It's burning and bursting into flames and the . . . and it's falling on the mooring mast, and all the folks agree that this is terrible; this is one of the worst catastrophes in the world. Oh, it's crashing . . . oh, four or five hundred feet into the sky, and it's a terrific crash, ladies and gentlemen. There's smoke, and there's flames, now, and the frame is crashing to the ground, not quite to the mooring mast. Oh, the humanity, and all the passengers screaming around here! I told you—I can't even talk to people, their friends are on there! Ah! It's . . . it . . . it's a . . . ah! I . . . I can't talk, ladies and gentlemen. Honest: it's just laying there, a mass of smoking wreckage. Ah! And everybody can hardly breathe and talk and the screaming. I . . . I . . . I'm sorry. Honest: I . . . I can hardly breathe. I . . . I'm going to step inside, where I cannot see it. Charlie, that's terrible. Ah, ah . . . I can't. Listen, folks; I . . . I'm gonna have to stop for a minute because I've lost my voice. This is the worst thing I've ever witnessed." Morrison's description of the disaster took less than a minute and a half. It is what most people remember about the event, those emotionally impactful seconds that brought the reporter to tears. What many don't know is that he quickly regained his composure and recorded almost 37 minutes of information reporting on rescue efforts and interviewing some of the witnesses of the crash that took the lives of 35 people and brought an end to the era of the great airships.

The Hindenburg *disaster*

Morrison's account was not a live broadcast. It was being recorded for a rebroadcast. After finishing their work, Morrison and Nehlsen rushed back to Chicago with the recordings but leaving their heavy equipment behind. The next day it was broadcast on WLS in Chicago with an excerpt aired on both the NBC Red and Blue networks that morning and once again in the afternoon. The NBC broadcast was significant because that network had a policy against airing recorded material. As such, Morrison's account was the first time a recording was broadcast by NBC. For years people claimed they had heard Morrison deliver a live account of the disaster, but in truth, no one ever did. The fact that many who heard it felt it was a live broadcast is a testament to the feelings Morrison's voice brought to the ears of a radio listener conveyed at the time.

A recent study of the technical details of the recording discovered that due to an error in the recording speed, the playback ran a little too fast, which caused the pitch in Morrison's voice to sound a bit high and squeaky. The fact is that Morrison had a mellow voice well suited to his position as a radio commentator. Decades after the event, Morrison's heartfelt coverage was paired with film footage and shown as a newsreel in movie theaters around the country. Many alive today learned about the disaster by viewing this pairing.

Those who have listened to all of Morrison's coverage of the event are virtually unanimous in concluding that he did his job well. He investigated an ongoing situation and was accurate in his descriptions. His 37-minute broadcast included interviews with witnesses and a surviving passenger who described his escape in German. Morrison also speculated that the crash might have been caused by static electricity resulting from the day's thunderstorm activity that had delayed the arrival of the great airship. While we will never know for sure what caused the disaster, static electricity remains as the most likely culprit.

When World War II broke out, Morrison served in the Army Air Corps. Later he became a reporter and the first news director at WTAE-TV in Pittsburgh. He also made three unsuccessful runs for Congress as a member of the Republican Party. He was also instrumental in developing a radio and television section at West Virginia University. A fellow

The grave of Herbert Morrison

employee at WTAE said that on occasion, Morrison would talk about the *Hindenburg*. "What struck me about him and that incident is he never got over it. He was beside himself on that recording. I think it always stayed with him. It followed him all his life."

Morrison passed away about seven months after entering the Sundale Nursing Home in Morgantown, West Virginia. His wife remembered him as a quiet and unassuming man who "was very proud that he was able to do that broadcast." He was laid to rest in the Scottdale, Pennsylvania, Cemetery.

19.

ARNOLD PALMER

"The King"

County: Westmorland • Town: Latrobe
Cremated ashes scattered at the Latrobe Country Club
346 Arnold Palmer Drive

It is not an exaggeration to say that no one popularized the game of golf in America and around the world more than this man. Not only was he one of the most talented men to ever swing a golf club, but he was also arguably the most charismatic. He loathed playing it safe, choosing to attack each course on every shot. In his career, he won 62 PGA Tour titles and had a total of 95 professional wins. He came out on top in seven of golf's major events and finished tantalizingly close in many others. In 1974 he became one of the original inductees into the World Golf Hall of Fame. His winning ways earned him the nickname that he shared with Elvis Presley, "The King." Golf fans referred to him merely as Arnie, and when people heard that name, everyone knew they were talking about Arnold Palmer.

Palmer was born on September 10, 1929, in Latrobe, Pennsylvania. His birthplace remained important to him throughout his life. He once remarked, "Latrobe isn't just the place where I'm from; it's who I am." His mother was Doris Morrison, and his father bore the name Milfred Jerome "Deacon" Palmer, whose close friends called him Deke. Palmer's parents had a profound effect on his life. In his biography, *Arnie: The Life of Arnold Palmer*, written by Tom Callahan, Palmer remembered his mother as a "gentle, generous person" who always stood up for him. His father is recalled as steel country Pennsylvania tough. When Deacon was

Arnold Palmer

a boy, he contracted polio. In those days, particularly in places like small towns in Pennsylvania, there weren't a lot of medical specialists available to aid such a patient through rehabilitation. Palmer's father taught himself to walk again and exercised his arms and upper body to the point that even though he might wobble on his deformed foot, no one viewed him as handicapped. Palmer recalled his father as being so tough that he refused to compliment him on his accomplishments. As the great South African golfer Gary Player recalled: "I think Arnold wanted nothing so much in life as his father's approval, and, for all that Arnie accomplished, I don't believe he ever completely got it." What he did get from his father was access to the game of golf and a drive to succeed.

Deacon Palmer taught his son the game he would popularize around the United States and beyond its borders. Deacon was the head professional and groundskeeper at the Latrobe Country Club. Palmer would accompany his father as he cared for the course, where he learned the game from his dad, whose job also provided a place for his son to hone his skills. Some members criticized the elder Palmer for teaching his son to hit the ball so hard. According to Tom Callahan, Deacon's philosophy was to knock the hell out of it, go and find it, then knock the hell out of it again. Years later, Palmer would remember, "Funny, I never did hit the ball hard enough to suit Pap." Still, by the time he was 12, he was hitting it hard enough to break 40 on the club's nine-hole course. He also won several caddy tournaments at the club, but his father refused to allow him to bring the trophies home, telling Palmer, "They were for other men's sons."

In his youth, one of Palmer's friends who also hailed from Latrobe was the man who eventually became America's favorite neighbor: Fred Rogers (See *Keystone Tombstones Volume Two*). Rogers was a year ahead of Palmer in school, and the two got to know each other in Palmer's words "pretty well." As for Rogers, he recalled Palmer as friendly and pointed to their interests in airplanes as something they shared. He recalled building model planes with Palmer and visits to the Latrobe airport (that Palmer would later purchase) where they would watch the planes take off and land and touch the planes on the ground. Palmer never lost his love of airplanes, and he eventually became an accomplished pilot.

After he graduated from Latrobe High School in 1947, Palmer was ranked the number two amateur golfer in the United States, and he had received partial golf scholarship offers from both Penn State and Pitt. The offers covered tuition but not room and board. A friend of Palmer's by the name of Bud Worsham had received a full scholarship to Wake Forest University in North Carolina. According to Palmer, Worsham told him, "I'll bet I could get you a full ride, too." Later Palmer recalled, "And I'll be damned if he didn't."

For the next three years, the young golfing duo was inseparable. Rooming together and playing on the University team. One evening Worsham invited Palmer to join him and a Wake Forest basketball player, Gene Scheer, at a dance in Durham, which at the time was only about twenty miles away from Wake Forest. Palmer declined and went to a movie instead. When he woke up the next morning, he noticed that his roommate's bed hadn't been used. He checked around, and Scheer hadn't returned as well. On the way to the dance, Worsham's 1939 Buick had left the road and flipped over into a stream, killing both occupants. Palmer was taken to the funeral home, where he identified the victims. In 1960 Palmer established the Buddy Worsham Memorial Scholarship That provides financial aid for members of the Wake Forest Varsity Golf Team.

Deeply affected by his roommate's passing, Palmer left college and joined the United States Coast Guard. He served for three years but found time to continue honing his golfing skills: first in Cape May, New Jersey, and then in Cleveland, Ohio, where, according to his biographer, he played a lakeside course where at times, the flags were frozen into the cups.

When his enlistment ended, Palmer returned to Wake Forest. He never actually graduated as he was a few credits shy of earning a diploma. He did win the Atlantic Coast Conference Golf Championship.

In 1954 Palmer participated in the United States Amateur Championship held in Detroit. He won the event and called that victory, "the turning point" in his life. He noted that winning that tournament gave him the confidence he needed to compete with the best in the game. At the conclusion of his winning match, Palmer embraced his mother and then sought out his father. Deacon approached his son and said, "You did pretty good, boy." According to his biographer, the compliment from his father poured over him like a sunrise. On November 17, 1954, Palmer announced that he was turning pro.

1954 turned out to be quite a year for Palmer. Over that Labor Day weekend, he played in Fred Waring's (See Keystone Tombstones Volume One) Bill Waite Memorial Tournament held at Shawnee on Delaware, Pennsylvania. One of the tournament hostesses was Winifred Walzer, who Palmer met at the event. Within a week, he asked her to marry him. As he presented the first-place trophy to Palmer, Waring made no secret of the engagement. The couple was married five days before Christmas and stayed together until Winnie's death 45 years later. They had two daughters. Palmer once remarked about how lucky he was to be a professional athlete married to a woman he could refer to as "Win."

Arnie's statue at his hometown airport

Palmer's first professional tour win came in August of 1955 when he finished on top of the leaderboard in the Canadian Open. He earned $2,400 for his efforts. In that initial year, he also played in Pro-Am events and non-PGA events. He later estimated that he made approximately $8,000 in his first year as a pro, which was enough to keep him and his new bride, now pregnant with their first child, going.

That initial year as a professional also saw him travel to Augusta, Georgia, to compete in his first Masters Tournament. He would recall that first trip to the fabled site as the "greatest thrill of my life. Winning the Masters became an immediate goal, and he would equate wanting to win the tournament with wanting to breathe. In 1955 he finished tied for tenth, earning $696 in the process.

When one considers the reverence Palmer felt for the Masters, it is appropriate that he won his first major title at Augusta. The year was 1958, and the Tuesday before the start of the tournament, Palmer and Dow Finsterwald teamed up against Jackie Burke and the great Ben Hogan in a practice round. Palmer didn't play well, but Finsterwald carried him to a win over their two competitors. After the round, Palmer was in the lunchroom when Hogan, who never showed a liking for Palmer, arrived with Burke and sat at a different table. Turning to his playing partner Hogan, making sure he was speaking loud enough for Palmer to hear, said, "How the hell did he get in the Masters?" Palmer ended up making Hogan gobble up those words when he won the tournament by one stroke over Doug Ford and Fred Hawkins. With that win, the young man from Latrobe emerged as one of the leading stars in the world of golf.

Another significant year for Palmer was 1960. He won nine tournaments, including his second Masters. He also recorded what may be his most well-known win, and the one which cemented his reputation as a player who, faced with a difficult shot, would hitch up his trousers and take chances. The scene was the United States Open Championship held at the Cherry Hills Country Club located near Denver, Colorado. In those days, the final 36 holes were played on Saturday, and after three rounds, Palmer was seven shots back tied for 15th place.

Before returning to the course to finish his final 18 holes, Palmer stopped in the lunchroom to grab a quick bite to eat. He sat down at a table that included a Pittsburgh sportswriter, who Palmer considered a friend, named Bob Drum. Palmer asked Drum how he thought he'd make out if he shot a 65 that afternoon. Drum answered it would do no good that he was out of the running. Palmer pointed out that a 65 would give him a four-round total of 280 and asked, "Doesn't 280 win Opens?" Drum may have added fuel to a growing fire when he responded that they do "when Hogan shoots them." The conversation ended with Palmer leaving his hamburger behind as he left the table in a huff, later saying, "I was hot."

Arriving at the first hole to start his final round, Palmer stood on the elevated tee of the par-four looking at the pin about 346 yards away. The hole hadn't been kind to him in the first three rounds as he carded a double bogey, a bogey, before making a par earlier in the day. Perhaps thinking back to a lesson he said he learned after winning his second Masters that "when you miss a conservative shot, you're in just as much trouble as when you miss a bold one," he pulled out his driver and decided to go for the green. His ball stopped about twenty feet from the hole. He missed the eagle put but made a birdie. After seven holes, he was six under par for the day and finished with a 65 for a total of 280. He won his only United States Open by two strokes over a twenty-year-old United States Amateur champion named Jack Nicklaus.

As was pointed out above, this was a significant year for Palmer. Perhaps the wisest and most pivotal decision he made was signing up as the first client with the pioneering sports agent Mark McCormick. McCormick saw something in Palmer that, in his view, made the golfer an excellent spokesman and quite marketable. He listed those positives as Palmer's good looks, his modest Latrobe background, his aggressiveness on the golf course, his presence in several exciting finishes in the early days of televised golf, and his affability. He could have shortened his explanation by merely saying that Palmer had the charisma to not only match but surpass many of the athletes at the time. While his golf skills eroded with age, his charisma never did. Talking about Palmer, Sam Snead once said, "He went to bed with charisma and woke up with more." Through the successful relationship with McCormick, Palmer would earn far more money off the golf course than he would ever earn on it throughout his illustrious career.

After winning the Masters and the United States Open, Palmer traveled to Scotland to play in the British Open. Such a trip was unusual for American pros since the travel expense was tremendous and the prize money was small. Palmer, however, felt that winning the British title would put him the class of his predecessors, including Bobby Jones and Hogan, who crossed the pond to claim the title. Though he lost by one stroke in 1960, he went on to win British Open Championships in both 1961 and 1962. Many view Palmer's participation in these tournaments as instrumental in the internationalization of the game of golf.

It was also 1960 when Palmer went to Rochester, New York, where the professional athlete of the year would be announced at the Hickok Belt banquet. Yankee sluggers Mickey Mantle and Roger Maris were present, as were the stars of the gridiron, including Sam Huff and Johnny Unitas. Maris was so surprised to see Palmer that he looked at him and said, "What the fuck are you doing here?" After being named the winner, Palmer leaned over and repeated the same phrase to Maris. The two became good friends.

From 1960 through 1963, Palmer dominated the sport, winning 29 PGA events. It was during this period that his fan base grew to the point that they were christened "Arnie's Army." This loyal group would follow Palmer from tee to green for 18 holes at every tournament. In 1967 he became the first golfer to amass a million dollars in career earnings. By that time, he was the eldest member of golf's big three, a trio that dominated the game and included Jack Nicklaus and Gary Player.

In the 1967 Open at Baltusrol Golf Club, located in New Jersey, Palmer and Nicklaus were tied after 54 holes. On the final day, Palmer carded a more than respectable 69, but Nicklaus shot a 65, and Palmer finished second. Later Palmer would recall that week as the time that the torch was passed, though this may have occurred earlier, as Palmer won his last major, fittingly at Augusta, in 1964. Even as he aged, he remained competitive, winning a PGA Tour event every year up until 1972. As a matter of fact, in 1971, he won four tournaments. Palmer recorded his last PGA in the 1973 Bob Hope Dessert Classic when he beat Nicklaus and Johnny Miller by two strokes.

Throughout his life, Palmer created a golf-related business career. The Palmer Course Design Company (later renamed Arnold Palmer Design Company) was formed in 1972. Palmer would eventually partner in the design of over 300 golf courses, which can be found in 25 different countries. In 1971 he purchased the Latrobe Country Club where he had gotten his golfing start. Arnold Palmer Enterprises managed his role as a commercial spokesman, endorsements, and other commercial ventures. He also produced the popular drink called the Arnold Palmer, which combines sweet iced tea and lemonade. Palmer was also instrumental in the founding of the Golf Channel.

When Palmer left the PGA Tour, he participated in the Senior Tour (now called the Champions Tour). He won ten events on the Senior Tour, including five major senior championships. It is not an exaggeration to say that Palmer's presence gave that tour credibility in its early years. Jack Nicklaus said, "I doubt the Senior Tour would have happened without Arnold. Nobody would have bought into it if he didn't buy into it."

In 1994 Palmer played in his final United States Open at the age of 64. It was held at the site where he had participated in his first Open forty-one years earlier. Located near Pittsburgh and not far from his birthplace, Palmer walked up the 18th fairway at the Oakmont Country Club, waving to the fans who still adored him. He would three-putt for a round of 81 and miss the cut. When he left an Open green for the last time, he had tears in his eyes. The members of Arnie's Army responded with a two-minute ovation. Ten years later, he repeated the scene at Augusta when he played in his 50th consecutive and final Masters. Beginning in 2007, he served as an honorary starter for the Masters. He was eventually joined by the other members of the big three, Nicklaus and Player, in hitting ceremonial tee shots to start the tournament that always had a special place in his heart.

In 2005 Palmer married his second wife, Kathleen Gawthrop, in a ceremony held in Hawaii. During the spring and summer months, the couple resided in Latrobe. For the rest of the year, they split time between Florida and California. The Palmer family welcomed Kit into the family, and she filled a void for Palmer he had felt since Winnie's passing.

In 2012 Palmer became the sixth athlete to be awarded the Congressional Gold Medal. The ceremony was held in Washington, D.C., and Jack Nicklaus was invited to be the main speaker at the event. The Golden Bear waxed eloquently in praise of his formal rival, who had become his good friend. He remembered being a fourteen-year-old boy and seeing Palmer for the first time. He recalled he had just played a practice round in preparation for the Ohio State Amateur title and that as he left the 18th green, it was pouring rain and there on the practice tee was one man hitting ball after ball into the driving rain. Nicklaus recalled being awed by the man's strength. He walked into the clubhouse and asked, who is that on the practice range? He was told that's our defending champion, Arnold Palmer. He told other stories about Palmer's generosity to him when he was a young player starting on the tour. Story after story followed, and Nicklaus ended each one with "that's the Arnold Palmer I'll never forget." He concluded his speech saying, "The game of golf has given much to Arnold Palmer, but he has given back so much more. For many years everyone in this room can say, 'I remember when Arnold Palmer deservedly received the Congressional Gold Medal.' I just hope they'll never forget why." When Palmer accepted this honor, he was five years removed from receiving the Presidential Medal of Freedom from George W. Bush. Bush said he awarded Palmer the honor not only

A marvelous display honoring Palmer at a local hotel

for his impact on American sport but also for his influence on the American character.

Arnold Palmer passed away on September 25, 2016, while awaiting heart surgery at the University of Pittsburgh Medical Center. His memorial service was held at Saint Vincent College in a church located about two miles away from the country club where he had learned the game. Generations of golfers, both men and women, were on hand to pay their respects, including America's Ryder Cup Champions, who brought the trophy they had just won in the past week. His ashes were spread on

Arnie's ashes were spread at the Latrobe Country Club

top of Winnie's by the ninth green at the Latrobe Country Club. As one would expect, many commented on his passing, including President Barack Obama who issued a statement that read, "From a humble start working at the local club in his beloved Latrobe, Pennsylvania, to superstardom as the face of golf around the globe, Arnold was the American Dream come to life . . . Today, Michelle and I stand with Arnie's Army in saluting the King."

20.

HERB PENNOCK

"The Squire of Kennett Square"

County: Chester • Town: Kennett Square
Buried at Union Hill Cemetery
424 North Union Street

Herb Pennock was a Hall of Fame baseball pitcher from Kennett Square, Pennsylvania, who won three World Series championships with the New York Yankees and was undefeated in the Fall Classic. He was a steady veteran presence on the mound at Yankee Stadium for the great Yankees teams of the 1920s. After his playing career, Pennock became the general manager of the Philadelphia Phillies and built the team that became the 1950 pennant-winning Whiz Kids. Unfortunately, Pennock died before his team experienced that success. During his tenure with Philadelphia, some say he was opposed to integrating baseball, the likely reason he has mostly faded into obscurity.

Herbert Jefferis Pennock was born on February 10, 1894, in Kennett Square, Chester County, Pennsylvania, a suburb of Philadelphia. Pennock's father, Theodore, and mother, Mary Louise (née Sharp), were of Scotch-Irish and Quaker lineage. Herb was the youngest of four children. The family was independently wealthy thanks to the recent sale of their road farm equipment business.

Young Pennock first attended the Westtown School, a Quaker institution, and later the Cedarcroft Boarding School, both in the Kennett Square area. He played for the baseball team at Cedarcroft, where he struggled as a first baseman. He was a weak hitter, and his throws naturally curved. His teammate, Albert Aloe, who was also a first baseman,

Herb Pennock pitching for the Yankees

implored with the coach that Pennock was a natural pitcher. When the team's pitcher failed to show one day, the coach put Pennock on the mound, and he reportedly struck out nineteen batters.

In 1910, at the age of 16, while pitching with Cedarcroft, Pennock's battery mate was catcher Earle Mack, the son of Connie Mack, the manager of the Philadelphia Athletics of the American League. Pennock threw a no-hitter to Mack, who tipped off his father about the young lefty. A dialogue began between the elder Mack and Pennock's father, who wanted Herb to go to college. When Mack signed Pennock in 1911 to play for the Atlantic City Collegian team in the Seashore League for $100 a month, Pennock's father demanded Herb play under an assumed name to protect his eligibility. However, when Pennock threw a no-hitter against the St. Louis Stars, a traveling Negro League team, Mack promised a call-up to the majors in 1912.

Early in 1912, Pennock pitched for the Wenonah Military Academy in New Jersey. Mack called and offered Pennock a spot on his bench with the Athletics. Pennock accepted, and on his second day at the park, made his debut against the Chicago White Sox. He earned his first major league save three days later when he pitched the final three scoreless innings against the Detroit Tigers who were fielding replacement players due to their protest regarding Ty Cobb's suspension. The A's won 24–2 that day in one of the strangest games in baseball history. Pennock, only 18, played the rest of the season sparingly and was the youngest player in the league at the time. The A's finished third that year, but the rookie learned a lot from his teammates, including Chief Bender, who taught him the screwball.

Though missing the heart of the 1913 season to illness, Pennock pitched down the stretch in relief and helped the A's to the American League pennant. The nineteen-year-old lefty then watched from the bench as veteran lefthander Eddie Plank clinched the World Series championship against the New York Giants at the Polo Grounds.

Mack used Pennock a lot more in 1914. Ace Jack Coombs was still ailing from a bout with typhus that nearly killed him the prior year. Pennock filled in admirably at age 20, winning eleven games to four losses and posting a 2.79 ERA in over 151 innings pitched. Mack's A's again won the American League pennant but fell to the Boston Braves in the World Series, four games to none. Pennock made one appearance in the Series, throwing three scoreless innings to no avail.

Thinking his perennial pennant winners on the verge of being washed up, Mack broke up his team for the 1915 season. Stars Chief Bender, Eddie Plank, Home Run Baker, and Jack Coombs were gone. Mack tapped Pennock to pitch Opening Day that season at only age 21. Herb did not disappoint, tossing a one-hit shutout against the Boston

Red Sox. The only hit that day was by Harry Hooper, who chopped a single with two outs in the ninth inning that Pennock could have fielded but let roll to Lajoie at second. Nap could not make the throw in time, resulting in an infield hit. Pennock finished April winning three of four starts, but the rest of the team was not playing well. When Pennock began to struggle in May, Mack began to become disenchanted with him, believing he "lacked ambition." With the A's in last place, Mack sold Pennock to the Boston Red Sox at the waiver price of only $2,500. For the rest of his life, Mack regarded this as his biggest mistake.

The Red Sox, with Babe Ruth as their star pitcher, beat the Philadelphia Phillies in the World Series that year. Pennock was used sparingly in relief in only nine games before being loaned to the Providence Grays of the International League, where he spent the rest of the season.

After the season, on October 28, 1915, Pennock married his high school sweetheart, Esther M. Freck. She was the younger sister of a childhood friend. Over the ensuing years, Esther attended spring training and traveled with her husband during the season. The Pennocks had two children: Jane, born 1920, and Joe, born 1925.

In 1916, the Red Sox again won the World Series, but Pennock spent most of the season with Buffalo in the International League. They finished second for the pennant in 1917 with Pennock in the bullpen the entire season. Discouraged with his baseball career, Pennock then enlisted in the Navy to serve in World War I and missed the entire 1918 season. However, he did reluctantly pitch for a Navy team that defeated members of the U.S. Army in an exhibition before British King George VI on the Fourth of July. He had not intended to pitch for Navy and was at sea when Navy officials who were gearing up for the game learned he was in the mid-Atlantic. They ordered the ship to turn around and deliver Pennock to England, where he pitched before 40,000 at Chelsea Stadium, beating Army 2–1 in ten innings. After the game, the Red Sox signed him to a new contract and promised him a spot in the rotation for the next season.

Pennock's career began to gain traction in 1919, at the age of 25. With teammate Babe Ruth in left field, Pennock led the team with 16 wins. He

Pennock and Babe Ruth about to go fox hunting at Pennock's estate

again led the team with 16 wins in 1920, but the Babe was now off to New York, triggering the infamous "Curse of the Bambino." Pennock's win totals slipped the next two seasons as the Red Sox remained mired in the second division. After the 1922 season, Pennock was traded to the New York Yankees for Norm McMillan, George Murray, Camp Skinner, and $50,000. At the time, Herb and Esther Pennock were about to leave San Francisco to start a thirty-day tour of East Asia with Herb Hunter's traveling all-stars. In celebration of the trade, the couple danced a jig on the pier.

There were high expectations for the Yankees in 1923. Many felt the team needed a left-handed pitcher to put them over the top and felt Pennock was the answer. Miller Huggins's team had won American League pennants in 1921 and 1922 but lost to the Giants in the World Series both times. Pennock was stellar in his first season in New York, winning 19 games in the regular season while leading the league in winning percentage. The six-foot Pennock was very slender and pitched at a slow pace, circling the mound, adjusting his pants, and tugging on his cap between pitches. His motion was described as graceful. Grantland Rice, the sportswriter, once wrote that Pennock pitched each game "with the ease and coolness of a practice session." Pennock threw curveballs rather than fastballs and never seemed to exert himself very much. He was known for his quirky sense of humor that kept his teammates loose.

Pennock later spoke about his two principles of pitching: observe the enemy and conserve energy. Some described his performances as "effortless throwing" and "poetry in motion." Bill Dickey, his batterymate in later seasons, once said, "You can catch Pennock sitting in a rocking chair." He developed three curveballs, with different arcs, and a tailing fastball, which he rarely threw for a strike. Pennock was also known to be a sharp observer of opposing hitters while waiting for his turn.

Manager Miller Huggins was careful with his use of the lefthander, slotting him second or third in the rotation rather than first. This meant Pennock did not face the opposition's ace most of the time. In fifteen years in the same league as Walter Johnson, one of the all-time greats, Pennock only faced him three times. His record against stars Johnson, Coveleski, and Grove was 7–9 over his career.

But, none of this mattered in October 1923. Huggins's strategy worked as the Yankees again faced the New York Giants in the World Series. Pennock won the second game and saved the fourth game two days later. He then earned the win in the decisive sixth game on October 15. Umpire Billy Evans described it as "the greatest pitching performance I have ever seen," as Pennock "had nothing." The exhausted lefty had scattered nine hits and was behind 4–1 at the end of the seventh inning when the Yankees roared back with five runs in the eighth. The Yankees, thanks in part to the gutsy dead armed Pennock, were champions for the first time.

Over the next five seasons, Pennock was at his peak, often pitching in relief between starts. He won 21 games in 1924, ranking second to Walter Johnson in the American League. Pennock finished in the top five in many pitching categories, but the Yankees lost the pennant to Johnson's Senators.

In 1925, the Yankees slipped to 7th in the American League as Babe Ruth suffered from intestinal abscesses and missed a third of the season. Pennock led the team in wins. But the Bambino was back strong in 1926, and Pennock had a career-high 26 wins. *The Sporting News* touted Pennock as "the best lefthander in the majors." In the 1926 World Series, Pennock started and won the first and fifth games and held the Cardinals scoreless in the final three innings of game seven. He and Pete Alexander exchanged zeros as the teams battled in a one-run ballgame. Unfortunately, the Yankee bats were quiet, and Pennock was denied a third win. The Yankees lost to the St. Louis Cardinals in seven games.

The 1927 Yankees, known as "Murderer's Row," have been called by many the greatest team ever. During the regular season, they won 110 of 154 games. Babe Ruth hit 60 home runs while Lou Gehrig batted in 173. Waite Hoyte led the team with 22 wins. Pennock was right behind him with 19. In the World Series, Pennock won Game 3, yielding only one run on three hits in a complete nine-inning effort. He did not allow a hit until the eighth. The Yankees swept the Pittsburgh Pirates.

In 1928, Pennock was having what might have been his best season. By early August, he was 17–6 with a 2.60 ERA. He had just thrown a complete-game shutout against the Red Sox when he had to shut down his arm, unable to lift it to comb his hair. Pennock missed the rest of the season. The Yankees, who were on a pace to surpass the 1927 team in wins, plummeted in the standings but hung onto the pennant. They then swept the St. Louis Cardinals in the World Series without the lefthander. Some described the Yankee pitching staff without Pennock as "a three-stringed ukulele."

During his peak six seasons from 1923 to 28, Herb Pennock won 115 games and lost only 57. He had an ERA of 3.03 ERA. Twice he led the American League in WHIP, led baseball in shutouts once, and received MVP votes for three straight seasons.

Pennock, now 35, was never the same again. While he pitched well in spurts, he lacked the overall consistency demonstrated in past seasons. In

1929, he topped 200 career wins, becoming only the third lefthander to pass that mark by that time. His manager, Miller Huggins, passed away suddenly near the end of the season. It was not until 1932, under manager Joe McCarthy, that the Yankees returned to the World Series. Said McCarthy of his aging lefthander, "I'm going to pitch (Herb) Pennock in spots this season—the tough ones." The Yankees beat the Cubs that year in the World Series, and Pennock saved two of the wins.

On a personal note, through these years, Pennock continued to invest his baseball salaries. He purchased a successful fox pelt business, built greenhouses, and collected antique furniture. He liked to ride horses and go on fox hunts. These peculiar habits plus the fact he never swore nor drank led to him being dubbed the "Squire of Kennett Square" and later "The Knight of Kennett Square."

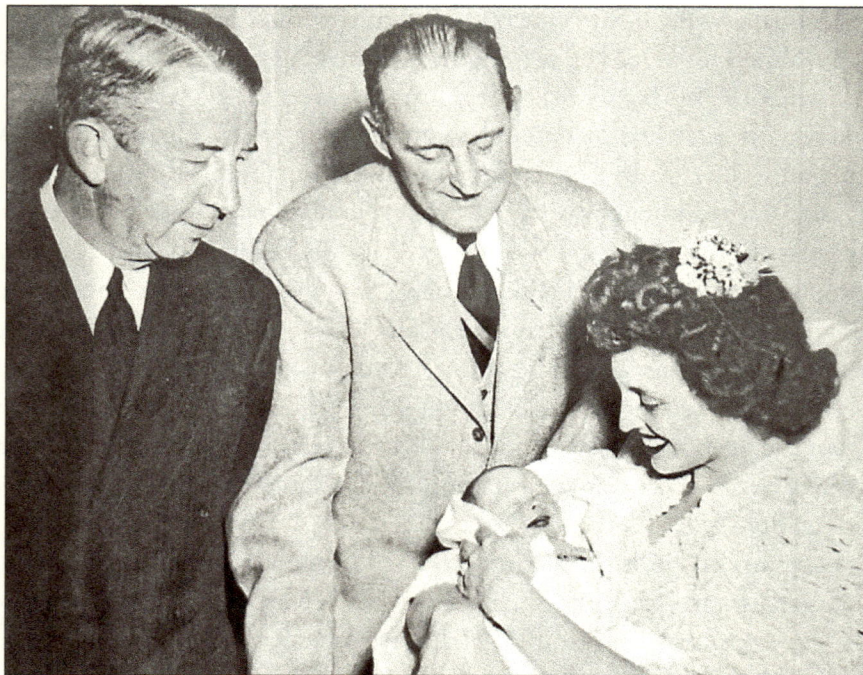

Herb Pennock with daughter Jane Collins, her husband Eddie Collins II, and baby Eddie III, the first grandson of two Hall of Famers

The 1933 season was Pennock's last with the Yankees. He was used in only 23 appearances, winning seven games. The Yankees failed to repeat as pennant winners. At 39, it appeared to be the end of the road for the crafty lefty. The Yankees honored him with a dinner on January 6, 1934, and then released him.

Pennock was not retired long, however. Former teammate and life-long friend Eddie Collins was the general manager of the Boston Red Sox. He signed Pennock for the 1934 season. Now 40, Pennock pitched mostly in relief, tallying 62 innings in 30 games.

Herb Pennock retired as a player with 241 wins against 162 losses and a 3.60 ERA. He pitched in five World Series and was a part of seven championship teams. In the World Series, he was undefeated, with five wins and three saves. Many considered him one of the greatest left-handed pitchers of all-time.

Pennock was not idle following his playing days. During 1935, he was the general manager of the Charlotte Hornets, a minor league team affiliated with the Red Sox. In 1936, Boston manager Joe Cronin pro-moted Pennock to first base and pitching coach for the major league team. He served in this capacity for three seasons. In 1939, he was the assistant supervisor of Boston's minor league system and succeeded his boss, Billy Evans, late in 1940.

The Phillies hired Pennock as their general manager in December 1943. The new owner, Ruly Carpenter Jr., had Pennock recommended to him by Connie Mack. Carpenter gave Pennock a lifetime contract, and he took over for the team owner while Carpenter served during World War II. Pennock was now working near where he grew up and began building what would become the pennant-winning Whiz Kids of 1950. Kennett Square honored him with Herb Pennock Day on April 30, 1944.

In 1947, during his tenure as the Phillies' general manager, Jackie Robinson was signed by the Brooklyn Dodgers. Harold Parrott, in his book *The Lords of Baseball*, claimed that he was listening in on an ex-tension line when Pennock called Branch Rickey of the Dodgers before Brooklyn was scheduled to arrive in Philadelphia and told him not to "bring that nigger here with the rest of the team." The caller further threatened to boycott a game if Robinson played. When the Dodgers came to town, they found their usual hotel unavailable, and the Phillies players and crowd treated Robinson viciously.

Keith Craig, in his 2016 book, *Herb Pennock: Baseball's Faultless Pitcher*, questioned whether the call ever happened. There were no telephone extension lines at that time, and there were no corroborating stories besides a sensationalized book written decades later. Craig also mentioned that the Pennocks had taken in a black woman who had been abused by her husband in the 1930s. The woman lived with their family for the rest of her life and was buried next to Pennock. Nevertheless, accusations of racism continue to this day against him.

Unfortunately for Pennock, he was never able to rehabilitate his reputation. Just months later, on January 30, 1948, he collapsed in the lobby of the Waldorf Astoria Hotel in New York and died of a cerebral hemorrhage. He was only 53 and seemed to be in perfect health. The outpouring of emotion was tremendous, The National League offered to cover the funeral, but the family preferred privacy. Regardless, hundreds of adoring fans, players, and executives passed Pennock's bier at the American Legion Hall in Kennett Square on February 3. Babe Ruth described his former teammate as a "honey of a pitcher who never made an enemy" and said his all-time, all-star pitching staff included Herb Pennock. Pennock was laid to rest that day at Union Hill Cemetery, survived by his wife, Esther, and children Joseph and Jane, who was the wife of Eddie Collins Jr.

Later in 1948, Herb Pennock was posthumously inducted into the Baseball Hall of Fame with 82% of the vote, despite having received much lower vote totals in previous years. However, an attempt to erect a statue in his honor in Kennett Square was blocked due to his alleged support of segregation.

In subsequent years, former teammate Fred Heimach referred to Pennock as the smartest ballplayer he ever knew. Lawrence Ritter and Donald Honig included Pennock in their 1981 book *The 100 Greatest Baseball Players of All Time*.

Some still write that Pennock is not deserving of the Hall of Fame due to alleged character issues and his overall numbers. While the Phillies team and fans treated Jackie Robinson horribly in 1948, there is no concrete proof that Pennock encouraged this behavior. The fact that it was Pennock who arranged the on-field handshake photo between Jackie Robinson and Phillies' manager Ben Chapman indicates he tried to mend the fence. There is more evidence that Pennock quietly tried to diffuse the situation between his good friend Chapman and the Dodgers without upsetting the team or the fans.

Regarding his numbers, according to the career pitcher WAR (wins above replacement) statistics believed to more accurately measure pitcher performance relative to the era and competition, as of this writing, Pennock is ranked 136th among starting pitchers. While representing a solid career, the numbers tell a story of someone on the fringe of consideration for the Hall of Fame. Chief Bender, Jack Morris, Catfish Hunter, Lefty Gomez, and Candy Cummings are the only Hall of Fame pitchers with weaker credentials. Curiously, directly above him in the rankings is a similar pitcher who did not make the Hall of Fame, yet, but was a World Series champion—Jamie Moyer from Sellersville, Pennsylvania— another crafty lefty from the suburbs of Philadelphia.

Pennock's grave

21.

HY LIT
AND
EDWARD SCIAKY
"Philadelphia DJs"

Counties: Montgomery and Delaware • Towns: Bala Cynwyd and Springfield
Lit is buried at West Laurel Hill Cemetery
225 Belmont Avenue
Sciaky is buried at Mount Sharon Cemetery
502 East Springfield Road

The city of Philadelphia, Pennsylvania, is home to a vibrant and rich musical heritage. Innovations in classical music, opera, R&B, jazz, and soul have earned the music of Philadelphia national and international renown.

The Philadelphia Orchestra's third conductor, Leopold Stokowski, championed American classical music, and in the animated film *Fantasia* brought traditional and modern classical music to a broad listening public for the first time. The Curtis Institute of Music on Rittenhouse Square has trained many of the world's best known and respected American composers and performers, including Leonard Bernstein. South Philadelphia native Marian Anderson was one of the most celebrated classical contraltos of the twentieth century. (See *Keystone Tombstones, Volume 3*, Chapter 2).

The city also produced innovative performers in rock and roll. The first national hit records featuring the blending of country and rhythm and blues—the essence of early rock and roll—came out of Philadelphia in 1953 and 1954.

Bill Haley, from Boothwyn near the city of Chester, worked as a disc jockey at Chester radio station WPWA and played in a group that performed with an innovative style. In May of 1954, they released a recording called "Rock Around The Clock." It didn't sell well. That summer Bill Haley and The Comets, as they had come to be called, had a huge hit called "Shake, Rattle, and Roll." That success led to a rediscovery of "Rock Around The Clock," which became a massive hit, and the group becoming rock and roll's first breakout artists.

American Bandstand, hosted by Dick Clark, became America's most influential outlet for youth pop music, started as a Philadelphia radio program, and was a local television show from 1952 to 1957 when it went national. Clark gave local acts a lot of important exposure. Local performers such as Frankie Avalon, Fabian, Bobby Rydell, The Dovells, Chubby Checker, and many others got important boosts from *Bandstand*.

As rock exploded, two Philadelphia DJs played important roles in the development of the music scene. The first was Hy Lit. He was there at the dawn of rock and roll and practically became an overnight sensation. He was born in south Philadelphia on May 20, 1934. He got his start in radio in an unusual way. He had just returned to Philadelphia after graduating in 1955 from Miami University and was playing basketball with the program director of WHAT, Charles O'Donnell. O'Donnell liked the sound of Lit's voice and invited him to appear on the station. He caught on there and soon went to WRCV and then in 1956 to WIBG. He dominated AM radio as "the Jet Jockey on Flight 99," which was the frequency for WIBG. His six to ten nightly shows earned a staggering 71 share of the radio listening audience and made Lit in demand at dance halls and night clubs across the Delaware Valley. He released several successful LP *Hall Of Fame* collections of music he played on the show. He also hosted his own nationally syndicated television program on WKBS, seen in over thirty cities, including Detroit, Cleveland, and San Francisco.

Lit was a very good looking man, and reportedly women fell all over him. His first wife was Miss Philadelphia of 1956 and then a Miss Universe contestant. He was touted as the most handsome DJ in the

Hy Lit

world. He made a lot of money doing record hops—some nights commuting between two high schools. He was famous for his memorable phrases such as "you know Hy, he don't lie (except now and then between six and ten)" or "choice not chance, go to a Hy Lit dance."

Known as Hyski to many, for some reason, he took to calling himself "Hyski-O-Roonie-McVouty-O-Zoot" on the air. When the Beatles made their first U.S. tour, they stayed at Lit's house since they couldn't find a hotel that could provide privacy. He was the master of ceremonies at shows with the Four Tops, The Beatles, The Rolling Stones, Elvis, and the Beach Boys, just to name a few.

In the late 70s, Lit toured with the Harlem Globetrotters as their master of ceremonies. He was involved in a famous controversy with rival Philadelphia DJ and radio celebrity Jerry Blavat (The Geater with the Heater). Both had oldies shows on rival stations, and both made a lot of money doing record hops and personal appearances. In 1981, Blavat was having dinner in south Philadelphia with a mob boss Steve Bouras and several others when Bouras was shot dead in a contract killing. In 1995, Blavat and Lit met on television to discuss a report that a mob informant Phil Leonetti claimed that in 1984 Blavat had asked Nicky Scarfo, Leonetti's mentor and uncle, to rub out Hy Lit for cutting into Blavat's record hop business. Blavat denied everything. Lit acted like it was all in the past.

Lit spent sixteen years with oldies radio station WOGL despite being diagnosed with Parkinson's disease. He became an outstanding spokesperson for the fight to cure Parkinson's.

He was inducted into the Broadcast Pioneers Hall Of Fame on November 21, 2003. He died on November 17, 2007, at Paoli Memorial Hospital of kidney failure and was buried at West Laurel Hill Cemetery.

Hy Lit's grave

Ed Sciaky

Another Philadelphia DJ legend was Ed Sciaky (pronounced Shock-ee). Sciaky was born in New York City on April 2, 1948, and raised in Philadelphia where he graduated from Central High School in 1965 and then from Temple University in 1968, where he majored in mathematics. His broadcasting career started at Temple's radio station, WRTI-FM, hosting a show called *The Bright Lights of Broadway*. He later added a Saturday night folk music show to his schedule.

His path and Hy Lit's crossed in an unusual way. Sciaky was a guest on a radio talk show. A caller asked him what he thought of current Philadelphia radio. His answer mentioned several radio stations, including WDAS-FM, which was home to *Hyski's Underground* at the time. He said WDAS needed lots of help. The caller then called Hy Lit and told him what Sciaky said. Hy Lit called immediately and discussed Sciaky's comments with him on the air. The result was that Lit invited Sciaky to WDAS and put him on the air for a live audition. Lit's wife called Lit during this and said, "are you listening to this guy? He's really, really good." Sciaky was hired at WDAS, Philadelphia's first full-time progressive rock station. He moved to WMMR in 1970.

He was one of the first FM disc jockeys who thrived when allowed to choose their music. He frequently played lesser-known songs. He befriended many musicians who enjoyed his intelligent interviews and knowledge. He featured a young Billy Joel on a famous broadcast from Philadelphia's well-known Sigma Sound Studio. He is credited with being the first to play Bruce Springsteen on the radio. The gregarious Sciaky and his wife Judy entertained many a musician at their home and were almost always backstage after shows. In Springsteen's early days, Bruce slept several nights on the Sciaky's green velvet sofa, forever after called the "Bruce Memorial Couch." Sciaky also earned Springsteen one of his first big paydays by persuading Manfred Mann to cover "Blinded by the Light," a million-plus seller that reached number one in 1977. In 2003, Sciaky's *Sundays with Springsteen* show won a Best of Philly award from *Philadelphia Magazine*.

Sciaky had a series of television shows on the PRISM cable service, and for several years was host of the *King Biscuit Flour Hour*, a syndicated radio program heard on over three hundred stations.

Ed Sciaky's grave

Ed Sciaky died suddenly on a street corner in New York City of complications from diabetes on January 29, 2004, at the age of 55. He was still hosting a weekly show on WMBK featuring the music of Bruce Springsteen.

"Ed Sciaky was the kind of DJ whose passion was the lifeblood for artists like myself," said Springsteen. "His support for my work brought me to an audience in Philadelphia that has remained one of my strongest to this day. He will be greatly missed."

Sciaky was posthumously inducted into the Broadcast Pioneers Hall of Fame in 2005.

He was buried at Mt. Sharon Cemetery in Springfield, Pennsylvania. "His passion for music influenced so many" is etched on his grave.

22.

JOSEPH PRIESTLEY

"Gunpowder Joe"

County: Northumberland • Town: Northumberland
Buried at Riverview Cemetery
7th and Orange Streets

Joseph Priestley was an English clergyman, political theorist, and physical scientist whose work contributed to advances in liberal political and religious thought and experimental chemistry. He is best remembered for his contribution to the chemistry of gases. He published over 150 works, invented carbonated water, and has been credited with the discovery of oxygen.

He was born into a family of moderately successful wool cloth makers in the Calvinist stronghold of West Riding, Yorkshire. He was the oldest of six children born to Mary Swift and Jonas Priestley. He was sent to live with his grandfather around the age of one to lighten the load on his mother. He returned home five years later after his mother died. When his father remarried in 1741, he was sent to live with his childless aunt and uncle. His aunt realized that he was precocious and sought the best education for the boy intending him for the ministry. As a result, young Priestley attended several local schools, where he learned Greek, Latin, and Hebrew.

In 1749, Priestley became seriously ill and was prevented from going to school. He continued his education at home. He taught himself French, Italian, algebra, and geometry and read the works of John Locke and Isaac Watts. The illness left him with a permanent stutter, and he gave up any thoughts of entering the ministry.

Joseph Priestley

In 1752 he entered the Dissenting Academy at Daventry. Dissenters, so named for their unwillingness to conform to the Church of England, were prevented by law from entering English universities. Because he had already read widely, he was allowed to skip the first two years of coursework. He received an excellent education at Daventry, enjoying the discipline and hard work and building warm friendships. He became what was known as a Rational Dissenter. Rational Dissenters abhor dogma and religious mysticism and emphasize the rational analysis of the natural world and the Bible. He renounced the Calvinist doctrines of original sin and atonement, and he rejected the Trinity. In his third year

Joseph Priestley's house in Northumberland

at Daventry, Priestley had a change of heart and committed himself to the ministry, which he described as "the noblest of all professions."

He graduated from Daventry in 1755 and moved to Needham Market, Suffolk, to minister at the local chapel. It was not a happy time as he struggled for money and to be accepted in the community. No one came to the school he established, and most were unable to accept his religious beliefs.

In 1758 he moved to Nantwich, Cheshire, and was much more successful ministering and establishing a school. He was unhappy with the quality of English grammar books, so he wrote his own, *The Rudiments of English Grammar*, which was exceptionally well received. The success of his school and book led to a teaching position at Warrington Academy in 1761.

Priestley moved to Warrington and assumed his duties as a tutor of modern languages and rhetoric. He fit in well there, and on June 23, 1762, he married Mary Wilkinson, the daughter of the famous ironmaster, Isaac Wilkinson. They had one daughter and three sons together.

His writings and lecturing at Warrington were very well received and popular. He designed two charts to serve as study aids for his lectures. These charts were, in fact, timelines and were popular for decades. The trustees of Warrington were so impressed they arranged for the University of Edinburgh to grant him a Doctor of Laws degree in 1764.

In 1767 Priestley left Warrington to become a minister for the Mill Hill Chapel in Leeds. The job paid more, and it allowed him to put the role of the ministry at the center of his life. Just before he left Warrington, Priestley had decided to write a history of electricity. Friends introduced him to the major experimenters in the field, including the visiting Ben Franklin. Franklin was very encouraging and urged Priestley to publish *The History and Present State of Electricity,* which he did in 1767. In this highly regarded work, he used history to show that scientific progress depended more on the accumulation of new facts that anyone could discover than on the theoretical insights of a few men of genius. This view of scientific methodology shaped Priestley's electrical experiments in which he anticipated the inverse square law of electrical attraction, discovered that charcoal conducted electricity, and noted the relationship between electricity and chemical change. Based on these experiments, he was elected a member of the Royal Society of London.

While in Leeds, Priestley started his three-volume *Institutes of Natural and Revealed Religion* in which he outlined his theories of religious instruction. It shocked and appalled many readers because it challenged basic Christian orthodoxies such as the divinity of Christ and the virgin birth.

In 1773 he moved to Calne, Wiltshire, to work as an aide to Lord Shelburne. He was given a house for his family and a good salary. Shelburne would later become Prime Minister in 1782. Priestley's years in Calne were the only ones in his life dominated by scientific investigations. During this time, he discovered oxygen, nitrogen, hydrochloric acid, ammonia, and carbon monoxide. He had invented soda-water (carbonation) in 1772.

In 1780 the Priestleys moved to Birmingham and he spent a happy decade as a minister, which he saw as the most crucial role in his life.

He made many friends and became a member of the prestigious Lunar Society, a group of prominent citizens devoted to science and its practical applications. In 1782 he published his *History of the Corruptions of Christianity* in which he rejected the Trinity, predestination, and the divine inspiration of the Bible. It upset many and brought a hailstorm of hostility his way. When he subsequently defended the French Revolution, he became seen as a subversive enemy of all accepted, conventional, decent opinions.

On July 14, 1791, Priestley and a group of followers met at a dinner to celebrate the second anniversary of the storming of the Bastille. Many opponents disapproved of the French Revolution and feared it might spread to Britain. They took this opportunity to start a full-scale riot. They burned the meeting house and the homes of many of Priestley's friends and supporters. Priestley's house and belongings were destroyed. After three days of what became known as the Priestley Riots, he moved to Hackney near London.

Priestley faced continuing pressure and the fear of further riots while he lived in London. He had to obtain official notice that he was not evading arrest before he could emigrate to the United States in 1794, where he hoped to find freedom and tolerance. The Priestleys arrived in New York City on June 4, 1794. They first lived in Philadelphia, where Priestley gave a series of sermons that led to the founding of the First Unitarian Church of Philadelphia and turned down an offer to teach chemistry at the University of Pennsylvania. While Priestley enjoyed preaching in Philadelphia, he could not afford to live there. He was determined to ensure the economic future of his family, and so he bought land and settled in Northumberland, Pennsylvania. He built a house and shared it with his son Joseph and his family. Before the house he was building was completed, his youngest son, Harry, died, probably from malaria. Then Mary died on September 17, 1796; she was already ill and never recovered from Harry's death.

Priestley continued with education projects that had always been important to him. He helped establish the Northumberland Academy, to which he donated his library. He exchanged letters with Thomas Jefferson

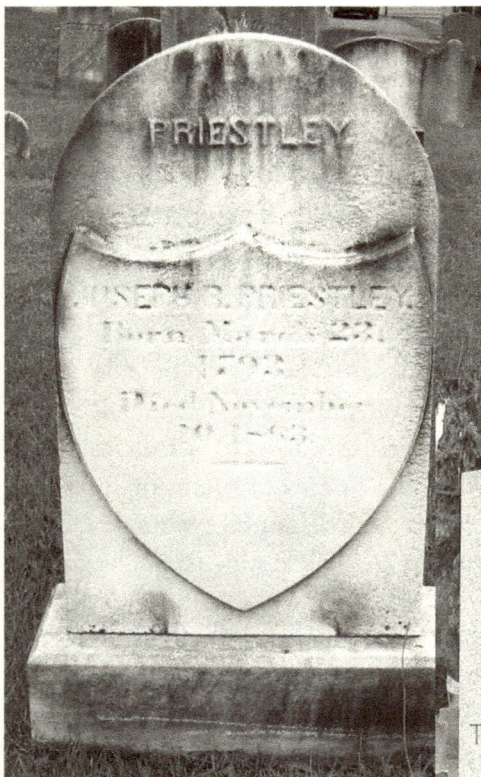

The initial gravestone for Priestley

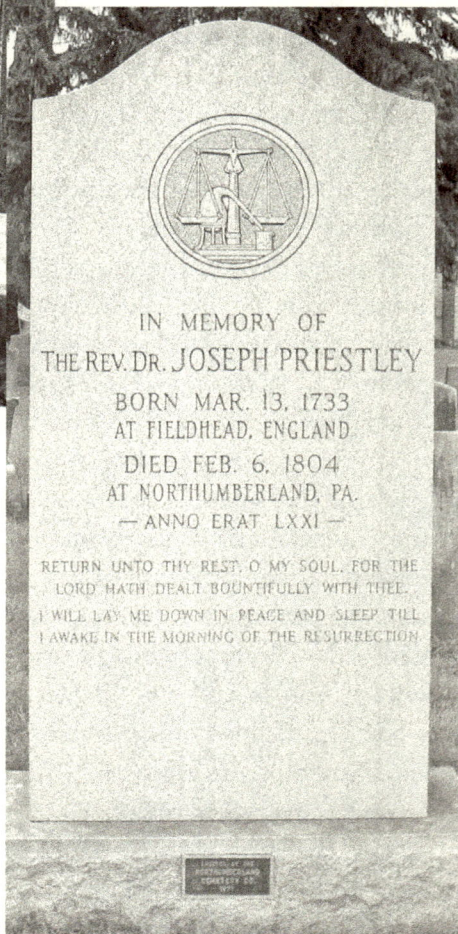

IN MEMORY OF
THE REV. DR. JOSEPH PRIESTLEY
BORN MAR. 13, 1733
AT FIELDHEAD, ENGLAND
DIED FEB. 6, 1804
AT NORTHUMBERLAND, PA.
— ANNO ERAT LXXI —

RETURN UNTO THY REST, O MY SOUL, FOR THE
LORD HATH DEALT BOUNTIFULLY WITH THEE.
I WILL LAY ME DOWN IN PEACE AND SLEEP TILL
I AWAKE IN THE MORNING OF THE RESURRECTION

An upgrade monument for Priestley

regarding the proper structure of a university, who used his ideas when founding the University of Virginia. They became close friends. Priestley dedicated one of his books, *General History of The Christian Church*, to President Jefferson. When Priestley became ill, Jefferson wrote to him that "Yours is one of the few lives precious to mankind, for the continuance of which every thinking man is solicitous."

Priestley tried to continue his scientific work in America with the support of the American Philosophical Society but was hampered by the lack of news from Europe of the latest developments.

In 1801 Priestley became ill, and his health continued a slow decline. He died on the morning of February 6, 1804, at the age of seventy.

Misunderstanding and miscommunication seem to be significant themes in Priestley's life. The ideas that he saw as reasonable and pleasing to God were seen by many as dangerously revolutionary in politics and religion. Although he regarded himself as a rational advocate of truth, his adversaries called him arrogant and incendiary. He was portrayed as a dangerous radical with a political and religious philosophy that would undermine the moral and social order. He was referred to as "Gunpowder Joe," an explosive enemy of church authority and the political status quo.

By the time he died, he had been made a member of every major scientific society in the western world. A marble statue of Priestley was unveiled in Birmingham, England, in 1874 to mark the 100th anniversary of Priestley's discovery of oxygen. Since 1952, Dickinson College in Carlisle, Pennsylvania, has bestowed the Joseph Priestley Award annually upon a distinguished scientist for notable contributions to humanity. His house in Northumberland has been designated a Historical Chemical Landmark by the American Chemical Society and a National Historic Landmark. The American Chemical Society also awards its highest honor, The Priestley Medal, in his name.

He is buried at Riverview Cemetery in Northumberland, Pennsylvania.

23.

171 VICTIMS

"Rhoads 'Opera House' Fire"

County: Berks • City: Boyertown
Buried at Fairview Cemetery
317 West Philadelphia Avenue

Though it was referred to as an "opera house" after the tragedy in Dr. Thomas J. B. Rhoads' building at the corner of Philadelphia Avenue and Washington Street in the center of Boyertown, Pennsylvania, it was not a grandiose theater as imagined. Rather, the three-story building included a meeting hall on the second floor, which could be rented to groups. This venue contained a small stage and was large enough to convene several hundred people. It was the chosen location by the local St. John's Lutheran Church for a performance of "The Scottish Reformation," a play depicting the death of Queen Mary, performed primarily by young parishioners on January 13, 1908. By the next morning, the bodies of 170 people, about ten percent of the town's population, were being removed to a nearby makeshift morgue, and a firefighter had lost his life.

This did not have to happen. The room only had one exit, and the doors opened in. The fire escape was not well-marked and could only be accessed by crawling out of the windows, which were over three feet above the floor. The fire could have been easily contained, if not for some errors in judgment. And, the crowd panicked, including the gentlemen, who, if they had been more heroic, would likely have saved most of the victims. Instead, what happened was a mad rush for the doors, which appeared to be locked or jammed, scores dying from the smoke and flames.

Photo of the burnt interior of the Rhoads building including some victims

Boyertown, Pennsylvania, in Edwardian times, was like many smaller cities in the region, bustling with economic activity and growing populations. The Model T had yet to be produced when the fire occurred, making it very likely most attendees arrived by trolley, horse-drawn carriage, or on foot, automobiles being relatively rare and expensive. In those days, the men wore derbies and jackets and ties. The ladies wore wide-brimmed hats and long-train dresses.

There were two performances scheduled for the play authored by Mrs. Harriet Earhart Monroe. The first was Monday evening, January 8. Another was booked for the following night. A total of 312 tickets were sold for the opening performance. It was estimated there were also over 60 people involved in the performance, including actors and stagehands from the church and local area. Mrs. Monroe was not present, but her sister, Mrs. Della Mayers, directed the play and had led the rehearsals. Monroe also provided the scripts, props, and costumes. The church and Mrs. Monroe planned to split the profits.

The initial two acts and first intermission went off without a hitch. During the second intermission, a young man, Harry Fisher, was working the stereopticon to project slides for a lecture by Mrs. Mayers about the historical background for the play. Said Fisher, an inexperienced

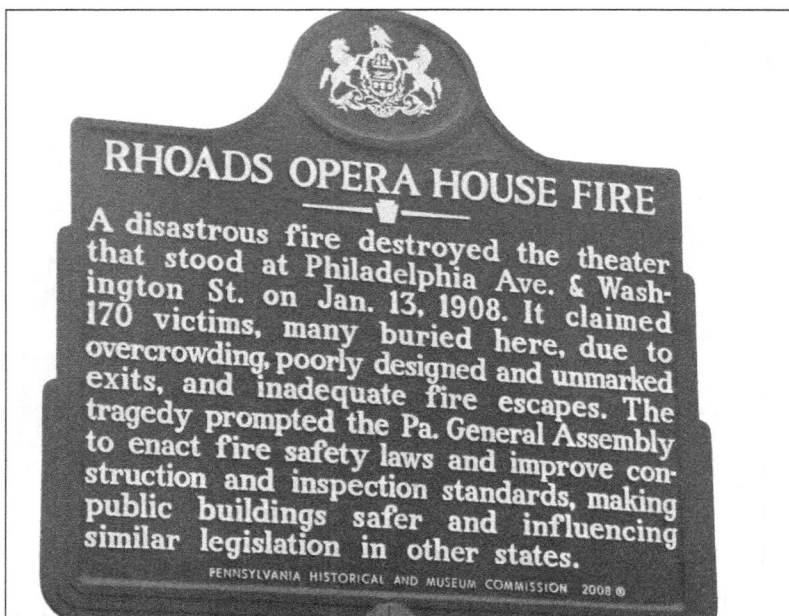

State historical marker in Boyertown at the cemetery

projectionist, in the *New York Times* a few days later, "I must have turned the wrong valve. There was a long-drawn-out hissing sound that frightened the women and children. Several of them jumped up and screamed and ran toward the stage. The curtain was down. I don't know what happened next."

The commotion in the audience caused several of the actors to peek from behind the muslin curtain to see what was going on. While doing so, someone inadvertently knocked over a kerosene lamp that had been sitting on the piano. This spilled flaming oil onto the front of the stage. Men in the crowd quickly reacted, and most in the room waited anxiously, as the fire on the stage was being put out. However, a couple of men, including the pastor, Reverand Adam M. Weber, attempted to move a tank of kerosene used to fuel the footlights away from the fire. This buckled the framework of the lights and caused more fuel to spill on the stage, reigniting the fire. Weber was severely burned by the mishap but called out to everyone urging "patience and unity." No one listened.

The rebuilt Rhoads building in downtown Boyertown, Pennsylvania

The inferno spread rapidly, first to the curtains, then to the wooden ceiling and wainscoting along the walls. Next, the gases emitted from the malfunctioning stereopticon caught fire. Everyone panicked and rushed for the exit, only to find the doors stuck due to the number of people pushing against them in the wrong direction. Parents grabbed their young children and tucked them under their arms as they darted about to find a way out.

"There was a wild rush for the exits. Everybody seemed to have lost control," recalled survivor Reuben Stover in the *Cranbury Press* a few days later. "The flames came towards the crowd like a great wave . . . once the crowd began to fight its way towards the doors, no power on earth could have saved all the lives."

Plaque on the wall of the rebuilt Rhoads building

In the ensuing chaos, people smashed windows, some finding the fire escape while others jumped two stories to the ground. Reverend Weber called out to his family, who were in the crowd, like many who had lost track of loved ones. The women's long dresses hampered their movements and were also very flammable.

Finally, one of the doors was splintered, resulting in a cascade of stampeding patrons who fell to their deaths or stumbled down the stairs. Rescuers were later horrified to find dead bodies piled five or six deep at the head of the narrow four-foot-wide staircase. "It was a terrible sight, and I shall carry the recollection as long as I live," continued Stover ". . . but I believe that, if the men had not lost control of themselves, the loss of life would have been very small."

"It was a battle in which only the strong had a chance to escape," Frank Cullen would later recall.

More than half of those in the building made it out. Reverend Weber was among the survivors but lost one of his young daughters. In some cases, entire families were lost. John Graver, a firefighter, was killed while responding to the incident. Della Earhart Mayers also died in the conflagration.

In his official report, the coroner would state that the victims included 110 females, forty-three males, and twelve whose sex was not distinguishable. The coroner noted that the flames had incinerated only the upper portions of the victims' bodies. The lower portions of the deceased had remained intact, clear evidence that fire had swept over the bunched-up victims, killing them while trapped against one another.

In *The New York Times* on January 14, 1908, Burgess Daniel Kohler of Boyertown stated, "Many of the men who perished in the fire were employed in the Boyertown Casket Company. The majority were carpenters employed in the making of coffins. Many a poor fellow unconsciously labored over the coffin in which he will be buried." In total, 171 perished, and 75 were seriously injured.

Fire companies from Boyertown and surrounding areas responded to the blaze, but it took many hours to get it under control. Finally, the

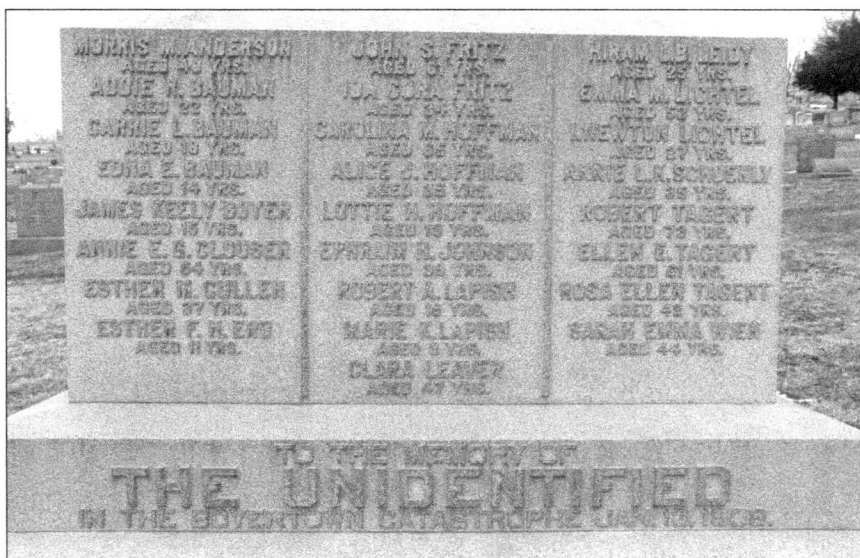

Large monument at the mass grave of the unidentified victims of the fire

next morning, the grim work of removing bodies began. The basement of a nearby saloon served as a morgue. Two other morgues were required, given the number of dead. Reports of missing persons were coordinated with identification activities.

News of the fire, the worst in Pennsylvania's history, spread to nearby towns, to Philadelphia, and across the nation. In the days immediately following the disaster, relief funds were received, and 107 new graves were dug at nearby Fairview Cemetery, including a mass grave for the 25 who were unknown. Over 15,000 people attended the funerals at Fairview Cemetery on one day. Others were buried in various cemeteries around the area, some as far away as Philadelphia and Lancaster.

By early 1909, the Pennsylvania legislature, with the signature of Governor Edwin Stuart, signed into law new standards for fire safety, including standards for exit signs, doors, lighting, extinguishers, and fire escapes.

Mrs. Monroe was the subject of lawsuits and was subpoenaed to appear before an official inquest, but declined to attend. She was exonerated

Grave of two victims named Boyer

from any blame. Monroe retired her play and lived until 1927, when she passed away in Washington, D.C. She and her sister were the paternal aunts of Amelia Earhart, the aviatrix.

Dr. Thomas Rhoads was arrested for criminal neglect but was later freed. He received insurance proceeds from the fire and had his building rebuilt on the spot only two years after the fire. This new building, which stands to this day, has slightly different features and interior design.

In 2008, honoring the 100th anniversary, Boyertown remembered the victims and this tragic event throughout the year. Historical markers can now be found at the building and cemetery, telling the tale of that fateful evening in 1908.

The Boyertown Area Historical Society at 45 South Chestnut Street contains an ongoing exhibit about the fire, including many gruesome photographs. It is a short walk, around the corner, from the site of fire. They are open on Tuesdays from 5 P.M. to 9 P.M., and Wednesdays from 9 A.M. to 4 P.M.

Durango's Saloon at 120 East Philadelphia Avenue is a couple of doors down from the former Rhoads building. The basement was used as a morgue during the fire. The Book Nook is a used bookstore on the first floor of 130 East Philadelphia Avenue, the location of the fire. Visiting the bookstore will allow you access to the interior of the building, which replaced the building involved in the fire. The upper floors have apartments for rent.

Grave of Stella Kolb a victim of the fire

24.

OWEN JOSEPHUS ROBERTS
"The Switch in Time That Saved Nine"

County: Chester • Town: Glenmoore
Buried at Saint Andrew's Episcopal Church
7 Saint Andrews Lane

In their 1936 book, *The Nine Old Men,* which covered the then-current members of the United States Supreme Court, Drew Pearson and Robert S. Allen titled his chapter "The Philadelphia Lawyer." Before his service on the court, he served in the office of the Philadelphia District Attorney. He then partnered in building a successful private law practice in the city of brotherly love. He was appointed by President Calvin Coolidge to serve as the Republican Special Counsel charged with investigating the Teapot Dome Scandal. He would later be appointed by President Franklin Delano Roosevelt to lead the fact-finding commission that investigated the surprise attack by the Japanese on Pearl Harbor. He served on the highest court in the land for fifteen years. His vote on the case involving a minimum wage law has been cited as a key factor that defeated a bill that would have allowed President Roosevelt to appoint additional judges more sympathetic to his policies to the Court. He would eventually resign from the Court and finish his career as the Dean of the University of Pennsylvania Law School. His name was Owen Josephus Roberts.

Roberts was born in Philadelphia on May 2, 1875. His father, Josephus Roberts, ran a successful hardware business. Upon retiring from the hardware business, he served as a Republican member of the Philadelphia Common Council, so his son was exposed to politics while

Justice Owen Roberts

still a boy. His mother came from Pennsylvania Dutch stock. The future Justice was educated at the private preparatory school Germantown Academy. He then attended the University of Pennsylvania, from which he received a bachelor's degree at the age of twenty in 1895. Three years later, he graduated from the university's law school at the top of his class.

His fellow students noted the abilities that may have aided him in the rise to the top of his class in their yearbook. They portrayed Roberts as a professor addressing his class saying "There is one practice of which, at the beginning of my college course, I resolved never to be guilty—the practice of gaining the goodwill of a professor by simulated interest in his words, by feigned zeal for his subject, by hypocritical amusement at his pleasantries. I refer to what is in common parlance known as 'leg-pulling.' As I said, I resolved never to be guilty of this."

In Philadelphia at the time, it was customary that established University of Pennsylvania alumni would lend a hand to the more recent graduates. John C. Bell was a former Penn football star who became an influential figure in the city's Republican Party. In 1903 he was appointed district attorney of Philadelphia. He decided to make Roberts his first assistant at a salary of $5,000 per year. Iz Durham, the Republican boss in the city, wouldn't hear of giving such a plum position to someone he viewed as a recent graduate who hadn't done enough work for the party. He told Bell, "A $5,000 job is a $5,000 job, and we're not going to stand for some student still wet behind the ears who never pulled a doorbell in his life and probably hasn't even voted. The appointment is out." Bell had to abandon the appointment, but he didn't abandon Roberts. He gave the young lawyer the title of special assistant without pay. After waiting a month, he slipped him on the regular payroll and, within the year, promoted him to the first assistant. Bell was even successful in getting the city council to provide back pay for the month Roberts had gone without a salary. Roberts made the most of his time in the district attorney's office, scoring many victories in the city's criminal courts. He was a handsome, energetic, hardworking, and quick-thinking young attorney who knew how to appeal to juries.

During this period Roberts also found time to marry Elizabeth Rogers, a woman who would support him throughout his career and is described in *The Nine Old Men* as a "charming, sometimes bullying little lady who has been Robert's pal, inspiration, and goad for thirty-two years, who reads his opinions, listens to him rehearse them, and on many important occasions has worn the pants in the Roberts family. Mrs. Roberts is ardently reactionary and doesn't care who knows it." The couple would produce one child, a daughter who they named after her mother.

Near the end of 1904, another Penn man, Charles Lemming, the chief counsel for the Philadelphia Rapid Transit Company, offered Roberts an opportunity to join his staff. Roberts left the district attorney's office and excelled yet again this time in representing the company in cases involving damage suits. In one case, a baker brought an action against the company when a streetcar smashed his wagon. The baker claimed he had injured his leg in the accident but refused to show the injury in court. Despite this, the baker was awarded damages totaling $3,500. A few years later, Roberts was back in court with a similar case involving a woman who fell from a streetcar after a sudden start. She claimed a leg injury that she also refused to show in court. During the jury selection process, the company found that five of the potential jurors had experience with accident cases. Roberts could only eliminate four, but he noted that one of the five was the baker who had prevailed years earlier. Going on the theory that the baker wouldn't allow someone else to get away with a scam as he had, he let the baker on the jury and won the case.

In March of 1914, Roberts and two other Philadelphia attorneys founded the law firm of Roberts, Montgomery & McKeehan. The firm thrived, representing the likes of the Pennsylvania Railroad and Bell Telephone. As the partnership grew, so did Roberts's fortune and reputation.

In 1924 President Coolidge was searching for someone to prosecute cases against those involved in the Teapot Dome Scandal. Many thought that Senator Tom Walsh of Montana, whose investigation had uncovered the scandal, would be the choice. President Coolidge didn't want Walsh in charge, and another University of Pennsylvania graduate came to the rescue. Pennsylvania Senator Gifford Pinchot and Penn alumnus Senator George Wharton Pepper recommended that the President name Roberts to the post. Coolidge agreed, and Roberts got the job.

By most accounts, Roberts performed admirably. In civil cases, he recovered all the property that had been stolen from the government. He also led the persecution in the successful case against former Secretary of the Interior Albert B. Fall, who was found guilty of accepting a $100,000 bribe. He did this while working for months without pay and while facing the high-powered defense teams employed by the oil industry. His debut in the national arena was covered nationally and marked him as one of the most well-known prosecutors at his time.

In 1930 President Herbert Hoover nominated Roberts to the Supreme Court after the Senate rejected his original choice, John J. Parker. He was confirmed and began his service on the court on May 20, 1930.

In his first two years on the court, Roberts aligned with the more liberal judges on the important cases. Things changed with the presidential election of Franklin Delano Roosevelt and the coming of the New Deal. For one thing, Roberts was a lifelong Republican, and his wife was an outspoken and ardent critic of the programs proposed by the new president. A fellow justice Pierce Butler also exerted an influence on Roberts. Butler sat next to Roberts on the court and became a frequent visitor to the Roberts home as he cemented a friendship aimed at wooing the younger justice to the conservative side.

Butler was a Minnesota Democrat who was nominated to the court by Warren Harding. Though he was a Democrat, he opposed the regulation of business, and most programs proposed and supported by President Roosevelt. His efforts bore fruit in 1936 when Roberts sided with the conservative judges in the case where the court ruled that the Agricultural Adjustment Act was unconstitutional. The ruling was viewed as a major blow to Roosevelt and his New Deal program. Robert's authored the opinion that held that the Act went beyond the taxing and spending powers that could be exercised by Congress. His opinion was broadly criticized by legal scholars, including Dr. Howard Lee McBain, professor of constitutional law at Columbia who stated, "One can hardly escape the conclusion that the Court was determined to kill this law no matter what sacrifice of logic and reasoning in the process of torturing the Constitution to that end," even supporters found it difficult to defend the decision. The very conservative ex-Senator David Aiken Reed said, "I agree with Mr. Robert's conclusions, but I wish to God he'd written a better opinion."

During this period, Roberts had considered leaving the Court to run for President. In the winter of 1935–36, Republicans were searching for a candidate to take on Roosevelt. Robert's name was prominent as a potential candidate. He was considered a healthy, handsome well-spoken, and highly regarded man with a record that included the prosecutions during Teapot Dome. It was thought that his Teapot Dome work would appeal to liberals. Besides, his home state of Pennsylvania had the second largest number of votes in the electoral college. According to Pearson and Allen, Mrs. Roberts decided for her husband, determining that it would be a mistake to enter the uncertain future that politics had to offer. Considering Roosevelt's subsequent landslide victory, it was probably the correct choice.

As it turned out, Roosevelt's smashing victory may have influenced an important vote that Roberts cast in the case of *West Coast Motel v. Parrish*, which upheld the constitutionality of minimum wage laws. Though Roosevelt had yet to put forth his plan to add additional justices to the court that would support his programs, Chief Justice Charles Evans Hughes was aware that the President was considering such a measure. Hughes was much relieved when Roberts agreed to vote with him and the three liberal judges on the minimum wage case. The Chief Justice reportedly congratulated Roberts telling him he had saved the court. Some have referred to Roberts's vote as "the switch in time that saved nine."

Roberts always disputed the notion that he had cast his vote in the minimum wage case to save the court. Years after Roberts died, Justice Felix Frankfurter contributed a tribute to a Roberts memorial issue of the *Penn Law Review.* Here Frankfurter made public a memo Roberts had sent him. In the memo, Roberts noted that he had cast his vote in the minimum wage case before Roosevelt announced his Court-packing plan. Roberts believed this evidence proved his vote had nothing to do with how he cast his vote. While true, what we do not know is whether or not Roberts had heard rumors or somehow gotten wind of the President's intentions. After leaving the Court, Roberts burned all his legal and judicial papers. As a result, the truth of the matter may never be known.

The same five judges stuck together in April of 1937 when they upheld the Constitutionality of the National Labor Relations Act. The decision validated a major New Deal program, the regulation of labor relations at the very time conflicts between labor and management were rocking the nation. Upon hearing the news, Roosevelt said, "Today is a very, very happy day." At the same time, the President raised the question as to whether he could continue to count on favorable opinions. He even cited a newspaperman who had observed that the court was now "Roberts's land." Roosevelt went through with his plan to pack the court. It failed. It is worth noting that Roberts also voted that the establishment of the Social Security fund was constitutional.

After the Japanese surprise attack on Pearl Harbor, Roosevelt appointed Roberts to head the commission assigned to investigate the "Day that will live in infamy" and took the country into World War II. An anti-war journalist called the appointment of Roberts a "masterstroke." According to John T. Flynn, "Roberts had been one of the most clamorous among those screaming for an open declaration of war." He concluded that Roberts would not cast any stain on the event that presented him with his wish. The subsequent report found that specific military commanders were derelict in their duty but laid no blame on what critics of the report called "high officials in Washington." Admiral Husband Kimmel was among those singled out for blame, and his descendants have been fighting for years to restore his honor.

In Roberts later years on the court, he became known as the leading dissenter by repeatedly expressing disagreement with the other justices, all of whom by this time had been appointed by Roosevelt. Many believe that the uneasy relationship with his colleagues led to his decision to

The grave of Owen Roberts

retire from the court in 1945. As an example of how poor Roberts's relationships had grown with his fellow justices, Justice Hugo Black refused to affix his signature to the letter that traditionally would have thanked Roberts for his service. The letter was modified to appease Black, but then the other justices refused to sign. As a result, no letter was sent.

After his retirement, Roberts served as the Dean of the University of Pennsylvania Law School from 1948 to 1951. He passed away at his farm located near Phoenixville, Pennsylvania, on May 17, 1955, at the age of eighty. He was laid to rest in a modest grave in Saint Andrew's Cemetery, located in Chester County. A school district near Pottstown, Pennsylvania, was named the Owen J. Roberts School District in his honor. Germantown Academy likewise honored his memory by naming their debate society after him.

25.

SHIKELLAMY

"Oneida Chief at Shamokin"

County: Northumberland • Town: Sunbury
Buried at the intersection of North Front Street
(State Highway 147) and Augusta Street

Shikellamy, also known as Swatana, was the vice-regent of the Six Nations of the Iroquois Confederacy, supervising the conquered Shawnee and Lenape (Delaware) tribes of central Pennsylvania at the juncture of the west and north branches of the Susquehanna River. This strategic location buttressed the southern border of the Six Nations and is the present-day site of the city of Sunbury, Pennsylvania, then known as Shamokin. It was also the crossroads for over half a dozen trails, including the Great Shamokin, Warriors, and Tulpehocken Paths. In his role, Shikellamy was strategically positioned to negotiate on behalf of the natives with the English and French. Through his friendship with Conrad Weiser, the interpreter from Womelsdorf, Pennsylvania, in western Berks County, the two worked to keep the peace during the decades before the French and Indian War. Known as "the Enlightened One" or "One who Enlightens Us," he was highly regarded by all whom he encountered.

It is not known precisely when Shikellamy was born, though some estimate 1688. Some say he was born at or near Oneida, New York, then the home of one of the Oneida tribe of the Iroquois Confederacy. Others say he was a member of another tribe, perhaps the Cayugas or Andastes, who was adopted by the Oneidas. Still, other legends say he was of French ancestry, captured at the age of two, and adopted by the Oneidas.

Modern bust of Shikellamy

Even if he wasn't a Cayuga, circa 1716, he married Neanoma, a member of that tribe. Their children, as was the tradition, subsequently claimed Cayuga heritage. The couple had four or five sons and at least one daughter. Tachnechtoris, "The Spreading Oak," was the oldest son. He was known to the English as John Shikellamy or Captain Logan in some records. Tah-gah-jute or Sayughtowa "The Beetling Brow" was better known as James Logan, in honor of the Secretary of the Provincial Council by that name, and later as Logan, the Mingo. Mingo was a derogatory term that referred to someone of mixed blood. The reference to his brow concerned his eyebrows that stuck out and over his forehead. The third son was Arahhot, who was probably the "Unhappy

Jake" mentioned in colonial records. He was killed in a battle with the Catawbas in 1744. Sogogeghyata, also known as John Petty, was the youngest brother who bore the name of an Indian trader in the area. A daughter was later the wife of Cajadies, who was known as "the best hunter among all the Indians." He died in November 1747, leaving her a widow. A fifth son is surmised in some records as another who was killed in battle.

Shikellamy is first mentioned in the historical record upon his 1728 visit to Philadelphia. He was said to live at "Shickellamy's Town" near the present town of Milton, Pennsylvania. Around this time, he had been sent by the Iroquois to oversee nearby Shamokin, which contained natives from several different tribes and, according to early European missionaries, was a lawless place that was difficult to govern. The Iroquois, based at Onondaga (modern-day Syracuse, New York), had conquered the

Early painting of Shikellamy

Susquehanna Valley during the 1600s. Shikellamy was sent to be their "eyes and ears."

Shikellamy kept his distance from the ruckus and did not touch alcohol. He said he never wished to be a fool. In later negotiations, he tried to prevent the sale of alcohol to the natives. He was well-respected by the natives and the colonials alike and treated many of the European visitors with kindness. He was invited back to Philadelphia in 1729 and was described as ". . . a trusty good man & great lover of the English."

184

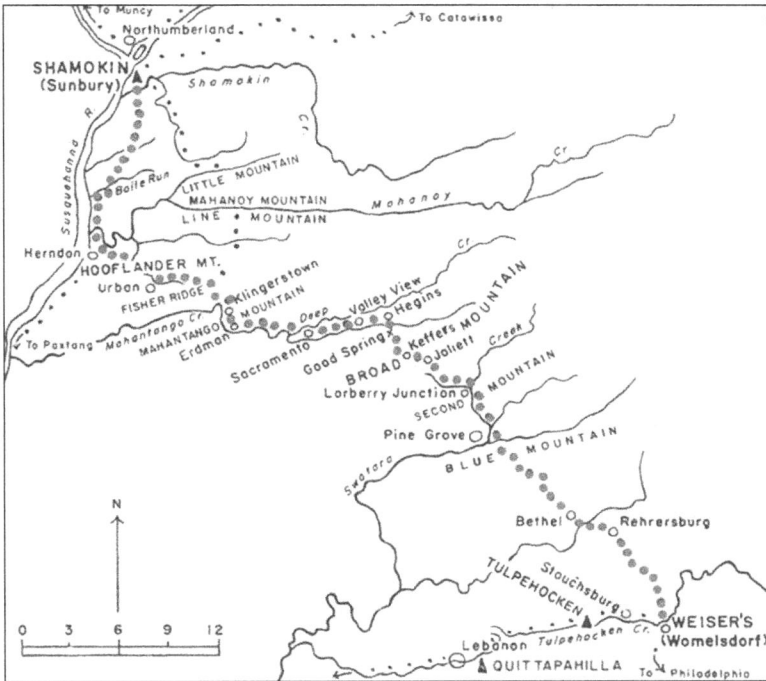

The Tulpehocken Path

Around 1731, he met the German settler Conrad Weiser who lived in modern-day Berks County, Pennsylvania and was a fluent speaker of the Iroquois dialect due to his experiences in his youth in upstate New York. Weiser lived along the Tulpehocken-Shamokin Path. The two became friends. Shikellamy asked Weiser to accompany him to Philadelphia as his interpreter. At the meeting, he warned the English to stop selling alcohol to the natives or risk losing their cooperation.

Worried that the Iroquois Confederacy might shift towards the French, Shikellamy and Weiser were sent to Onondaga on behalf of the colony to organize a council in 1732. It was the first of many journeys together that each referred to as "The Chain of Friendship," which helped cement the peace in the colonies before the French and Indian War.

Though the duo could only muster three of the Six Nations to attend the council in 1732, they managed to negotiate a settlement that kept the Six Nations with the English despite overtures from the French in Canada.

In 1736, Shikellamy, Weiser, and the Pennsylvanians met with delegates from all the Six Nations in Philadelphia. Over one hundred Iroquois delegates were present. The result of the meeting was the Treaty of 1736, granting all the land drained by the Delaware River and south of the Blue Mountain, including the Susquehanna Valley, to the colony. This was land the Iroquois had not occupied but had belonged to the conquered Lenape (Delaware) and other allied tribes. This was the first time the Penns had sided with just the Iroquois rather than negotiating with all parties. This was a deviation from the policies of William Penn, who had died in 1718. Some say this act later pushed the Lenape and others towards an alliance with the French.

The subsequent Walking Purchase of 1737, also arranged with Shikellamy and Weiser, provided more land in northeastern Pennsylvania to the Penns while also further alienating the Lenape and Shawnee but strengthening the ties with the Six Nations.

When the Shawnee moved west in 1742, Shikellamy moved to the village of Shamokin, which was then home to the recognized Lenape chief Sasoonan, also known as Allumapees. During 1742, Count Zinzendorf, a Moravian missionary from Germany, visited Shamokin. By this time, Shikellamy had converted to Christianity, and Zinzendorf hoped he could be useful in converting more of the natives to the faith. Shikellamy permitted the Moravians to maintain an outpost, including a blacksmith, at Shamokin, and he represented them at Madame Montour's village of Otstonwakin and French Margaret's village at the mouth of the Lycoming Creek. He helped build their houses at Shamokin and lent them horses because he knew they would not furnish alcohol to the natives.

Two years later, in 1744, Shikellamy and Weiser helped broker the Lancaster Treaty, an important settlement negotiated between the Six Nations and the colonies of Pennsylvania, Maryland, and Virginia. The terms of the agreement helped settle boundary disputes between Pennsylvania and Maryland. Because of Shikellamy's steadfast friendship with Weiser and the Pennsylvanians, the disputes were primarily settled

Statue of Shikellamy at the Conrad Weiser Homestead

in their favor. Nearly 250 Indians, including many squaws and children, had converged on Lancaster for the council, which proved to be one of the most consequential during colonial times while King George's War raged between England and France.

Following the treaty, Conrad Weiser oversaw the construction of a large house for Shikellamy at Shamokin that was nearly fifty feet long, upon pillars for safety, and covered with a shingle roof. Shikellamy would shut himself in when a drunken frolic was raging in the town.

In Bethlehem, a Moravian town, Shikellamy formally converted to Christianity in November 1748. On his way home, traveling with Bishop Zeisberger, he became ill with a fever at Tulpehocken. He barely made it back with assistance from his fellow travelers and died at Shamokin on December 6, 1748. Said Count Zinzendorf, of Shikellamy, "He was truly an excellent and good man, possessed of many noble qualities of mind, that would do honor to many white men, laying claims to refinement and intelligence. He possessed of great dignity, sobriety, and prudence, and was particularly noted for his extreme kindness to the inhabitants with whom he came in contact."

Bishop Zeisberger and Henry Frye built a coffin for the vice-regent. The local natives painted the deceased in bright colors and adorned him with many ornaments and his weapons before he was buried during a Christian service conducted by the bishop. The sachem was laid to rest in the traditional burying ground in the village by a large buttonwood tree that survived into the early 1900s. This spot is now mostly covered by a parking lot and a residential area.

After Shikellamy's death, his eldest son, known as John Shikellamy, succeeded him. However, historians disagree whether or not it was John or his brother James Logan who later became known as Chief Logan and was involved in Dunmore's War in 1774. Chief Logan issued an oft-quoted speech known as "Logan's Lament."

Shamokin, the Indian village, did not last for long after Shikellamy's death. With the fur trade shifting into the Ohio country and other land deals with Pennsylvania, the population was uprooted. During the French and Indian War, Fort Augusta was erected by the colonists on the site.

In 1858, a local man, Martin Hendricks, was digging in the location of the Indian burial ground and unearthed a wooden coffin containing the bones and relics belonging to Shikellamy. The remnants, including beads and a medal, passed through many hands until donated to the Northumberland County Historical Society, where they were displayed

Shikellamy's grave in downtown Sunbury

in the early 1990s. It is not known what happened to the bones, but it is assumed they were returned to the grave. Out of respect for Native Americans, the artifacts are no longer displayed.

In 1915, a stone memorial was erected to Shikellamy on the upper end of Sunbury near his gravesite. On it is a bronze plaque inscribed with the following:

Erected as a memorial to Shikellamy, also Swataney, "Our Enlightener," the representative of the Six Nations, in this province. First sent to Shamokin 'Sunbury' in 1728. Appointed Vice-Regent in 1745, died December 6, 1748. He was buried near this spot. This diplomat and statesman was a firm friend of the Province of Pennsylvania—erected by Augusta Chapter D. A. R. in cooperation with Pennsylvania Historical Commission, June 1915.

Shikellamy's name is prominent throughout the greater Sunbury area. There is Shikellamy State Park, High School, and Elementary School. The schools mentioned are part of the Shikellamy School District. Until 1978, there was a Boy Scout camp in Berks County named for him. There is an outlook on the Appalachian Trail named for him. There is also a statue at the Conrad Weiser homestead honoring him.

Had Shikellamy and Weiser not been friends and collaborated peacefully for the nearly twenty years before the French and Indian War, it is very likely the history of Pennsylvania, and possibly the United States would have been very different.

26.

FREDERICK TAYLOR

"Father of Scientific Management"

County: Montgomery • Town: Bala Cynwyd
Buried at West Laurel Hill Cemetery
225 Belmont Avenue

Frederick Taylor was the originator of the modern scientific management movement. His writings and lectures formed the basis of the reorganization of methods of handling labor in many of the largest industries in the country. His life's work was chiefly devoted to the simplification of industrial processes to reduce cost and increase outputs. His impact on the modern world has been significant. In 2001, the Fellows of The Academy of Management voted Taylor's *The Principles of Scientific Management* the most influential management book of the twentieth century.

Frederick Taylor was born into a Quaker family on March 20, 1856, in Philadelphia, Pennsylvania. His father was a Princeton-educated lawyer, and his mother, Emily Annette Taylor, was an ardent abolitionist and a friend and coworker of Lucretia Mott.

At the age of 16, after a three-year trip through Europe, he entered Phillips Exeter Academy in New Hampshire with a plan to go to Harvard and become a lawyer like his father. He graduated first in his class and captained the baseball team. In 1874 he passed the entrance exam for Harvard but was forced to change plans as his eyesight was rapidly deteriorating. Instead, he took the unusual step for someone of his upper-class background of becoming an apprentice patternmaker and machinist at the Enterprise Hydraulic Works, a pump manufacturing company. There he finished his four-year apprenticeship and, in 1878,

Frederick Taylor

became a machine-shop laborer at Midvale Steel Works in Philadelphia. He was successively gang boss, assistant foreman, foreman of the machine shop, master mechanic, chief draftsman, and chief engineer. His fast rise reflected both his talent and his family's relationship with part-owner Edward Clark. Taylor's sister was married to Clark's son.

Early on at Midvale, Taylor recognized that workers were not working their machines or themselves nearly as hard as they could. Called "soldiering," this behavior resulted in higher labor costs for the company.

To determine how much work to expect, he began to analyze the productivity of men and machines. His focus on the human component of production he labeled "scientific management."

192

Around this time, he persuaded Stevens Institute, in Hoboken, New Jersey, to let him take its regular course in mechanical engineering on a home-study basis. Since he worked six or sometimes seven days a week, he had to study at night or in the wee hours of the morning.

While doing all this, he somehow found the time to win the first tennis doubles tournament in the 1881 US National Championships, the precursor of the US Open. His partner was Clarence Clark, his brother-in-law. In 1883 he obtained his degree in Mechanical Engineering from the Stevens Institute of Technology, and the following year married Louise Spooner of Philadelphia.

It was at Midvale that Taylor introduced time study. The profession of time study was founded on the success of this project, which also formed the basis of Taylor's subsequent theories of management science. He suggested that efficiency in a shop or factory could be greatly enhanced by close observation of the individual workers and the elimination of wasted time and motion. He believed in finding the right jobs for workers and then paying them well for their increased output. He advocated paying the person and not the job and thought that unions would be unnecessary if workers were paid their worth. Taylor doubled productivity at Midvale.

In 1890 Taylor became general manager of the Manufacturing Investment Company and created the new profession of management consulting. He served many prominent firms, including Bethlehem Steel, where he implemented production planning, real-time analysis of daily output and costs, and a modern accounting system.

While at Bethlehem Steel, he developed the best known and most profitable of his more than forty patents. The Taylor-White process for treating tool steel revolutionized metal cutting techniques and brought Taylor international recognition.

Taylor retired at age forty-five but continued to devote time and money to promote the principles of scientific management through lectures at universities and professional societies. The American Society of Mechanical Engineers elected him their president in 1906, the same year in which the University of Pennsylvania awarded him an honorary doctor of science degree.

Despite all these successes and honors, Taylor's work was rarely known outside of the engineering world until a lawyer and future US Supreme Court Justice Louis Brandeis used his ideas in the Interstate Commerce Commission (ICC) hearings concerning railroad rates. He used Taylor's scientific management methods as an example of progressive management techniques that could ease the strain on workers even as it raised their pay and increased profits for owners. Brandeis argued that wage increases did not necessitate increases in railroad rates. He argued that properly managed railroads, that is those managed according to the principles of Taylor, did not need to raise rates to increase wages. *The Eastern Rate Case*, as it became known, stimulated a great deal of interest in notions of efficiency. Brandeis argued that the Eastern Railroad Company was seeking a rate hike because of failed management, and the cost of poor management shouldn't be passed on to the public. When the ICC asked him to propose a cure for the ailment that Eastern Railroad was suffering from, Brandeis recommended: "scientific management" (the term he coined after Taylor's system). The ICC summoned Taylor, who, in his testimony, explained how it could increase efficiency in various business operations. The ICC ruled that improvements in management were possible and must be made before the need for rate relief would be recognized.

In 1911, Taylor's classic *The Principles of Scientific Management* was published. His ideas were an accumulation of his life's work. Scientific management is the theory that analyzes and synthesizes workflow to improve economic efficiency. It contained four principles:

1. Each part of an individual's work is analyzed "scientifically," and the most efficient method for undertaking the job is devised; the one best way of working. This consists of examining the implements needed to carry out the work and measuring the maximum amount a first-class worker could do in a day. Workers are then expected to do this much work every day.
2. The most suitable person to undertake the job is chosen, again scientifically. The individual is taught to do the job in the exact

way devised. It is management's role to find out which job suited each employee and then train them until they are first class.

3. Provide detailed instruction and supervision of each worker in the performance of that worker's task.
4. There is a clear "division" of work and responsibility between management and workers. Managers concern themselves with the planning and supervision of the work, and workers carry it out.

Taylor is also remembered for developing the stopwatch time study, which, combined with Frank Gilbreth's motion study methods, later became the field of time and motion study. His fame increased further after his testimony in 1912 at hearings conducted by a select committee of the US House of Representatives to investigate scientific management and its influence on the workplace.

The grave of Frederick Taylor

In the early spring of 1915, Frederick Taylor caught pneumonia and died on March 21, at the age of 59. He was buried in West Laurel Hill Cemetery in Bala Cynwyd, Pennsylvania.

Sixty years later, Peter Drucker, America's guru of management, had this to say: "Frederick W. Taylor was the first man in recorded history who deemed work deserving of systematic observation and study. On Taylor's scientific management rests, above all, the tremendous surge of affluence in the last seventy-five years which has lifted the working masses in the developed countries well above any level recorded before, even for the well-to-do. Taylor, though the Issac Newton of the science of work, laid only first foundations, however. Not much has been added to them since-even though he has been dead all of sixty years."

27.

THEODORE "DUTCH" VAN KIRK

"'Little Boy' Blew"

County: Northumberland • Town: Northumberland
Buried at Riverview Cemetery
7th and Orange Streets

At approximately 8:15 A.M. on August 6, 1945, the bomb bay doors opened on the B-29 Superfortress *Enola Gay*, releasing the world's first atomic weapon dubbed "Little Boy" above the Japanese city of Hiroshima. The resulting explosion and mushroom cloud signified the closing days of World War II and the dawning of the Atomic Age fraught with the looming Cold War and fears of mutually assured destruction.

This Special Mission 13 of the 393rd Bombardment Squadron included seven aircraft and dozens of men led by Colonel Paul Tibbetts, who piloted the *Enola Gay*, which was responsible for delivering the weapon. Among the crew on board with "Little Boy" was bombardier Major Tom Ferebee and a twenty-four-year-old captain from Pennsylvania named Theodore "Dutch" Van Kirk, who had been selected to navigate the lead plane to the target.

Theodore Jerome Van Kirk, called Ted or Teddy by his family, was born February 27, 1921, in Northumberland, Pennsylvania, a small town across the Susquehanna River from Sunbury. His father, Frederick F. Van Kirk (1901–1969), and mother, Grace Florence Snyder Van Kirk (1901–1944), raised Theodore and his sister, Jean, born 1926, through the Great Depression when the children attended Northumberland High School. The elder Van Kirk was in the employ of Weis Markets for over

Major Theodore "Dutch" Van Kirk

thirty years, at one time as a cargo truck driver who made daily runs to Centre County.

After Ted graduated from high school in 1939, he attended Susquehanna University in nearby Selinsgrove. During those years, he had grown very fond of a young lady named Mary Jane Young with whom he had attended high school.

In October 1941, with the threat of war on the horizon, Ted dropped out of college to join the Army Air Force Aviation Cadet Program to become a pilot. Now away from Mary Jane, the couple wrote many letters to each other over the ensuing years, some of which are available in the book *My True Course: Dutch Van Kirk, Northumberland to Hiroshima.* Mother Grace also wrote letters nearly every day to her son, many of which are highlighted in the book.

The following year, Van Kirk received his commission and navigator wings and was transferred to England as part of the 97th Bomb Group, the first B-17 Flying Fortress unit there. Around this time, Mary Jane also saw her four brothers and their high school classmate, William J. Kelley, head off to war. Kelley later stormed the beach at Iwo Jima.

Assigned to the B-17 dubbed *Red Gremlin*, Van Kirk served with pilot Paul Tibbets and bombardier Tom Ferebee for 57 bombing missions over Germany or German-held territory. For eleven of those missions from August to October 1942, they were the lead aircraft responsible for navigation. Many sources note the risk involved in flying in these missions. Over fifty percent of the crews were eventually lost. More men of the 8th Air Force in Europe were lost than Marines in the Pacific during World War II. A typical bomber had a ten percent chance of being shot down in the early days of the war. By the tenth mission, the crews were on borrowed time.

Tibbets and his crew were selected to fly a secret mission to North Africa in October 1942. Their passenger was General Mark Clark, who was to rendezvous with the French before Operation Torch. The next month, they ferried General Eisenhower to Gibraltar, where he commanded the North African invasion forces. Clearly, the brass saw Tibbets and his crew as top-notch.

As the Germans began reinforcing in North Africa through the port of Bizerte, Tunisia, the Allied forces were threatened. On November 16, 1942, Tibbets and his crew led a surprise bombing attack on Sidi Ahmed Air Base at Bizerte, disrupting this key supply line with Axis forces in nearby Sicily and the Italian mainland.

It was policy in the Army Air Force to limit the crews to fifty missions, at which point they would be sent stateside. Tibbets and his crew exceeded this number and were finally returned to the U.S.A. in June 1943, Van Kirk serving as an instructor navigator at Selman Army Airfield near Monroe, Louisiana. Later that year, on September 16, Mary Jane Young joined him there, and the two were married at the parsonage of the First Baptist Church in Shreveport. Not long after, Van Kirk was promoted to captain.

Three officers of the Enola Gay: Captain Ted Van Kirk, navigator; Colonel Paul W. Tibbets, Jr., pilot; Major Thomas W. Ferebee, bombardier

During the week of February 7, 1944, Theodore's mother, Grace, fell and broke her arm at home. She had been sickly for a while with kidney disease and was treated for the broken bone. Three days later, she arrived at the hospital again and died within the hour of complications from her fall and her kidney disease. She has only 42 years old. Newlyweds Ted and Mary Jane received word in Louisiana and returned to Pennsylvania for the funeral. The loss most impacted father Fred and sister Jean. The Van Kirks did not have health insurance, and it took Fred many months to pay the bills. Concerned about Jean keeping house as a teenager while he worked long hours, Fred downsized to an apartment.

Late in 1944, Van Kirk was reunited with Tibbets and Ferebee at Wendover Field, Utah, as part of the 509th Composite Group, specially formed to handle nuclear weapons. Van Kirk later recalled being recruited by Tibbets for the group. "He told me, 'We're going to do something that I can't tell you about right now, but if it works, it will end

The Enola Gay, a B-29 Superfortress

or significantly shorten the war.' And I thought, 'Oh, yeah, buddy, I've heard that before.'" The crew trained for many months in preparation for the potential use of the first atomic bomb built during the top-secret Manhattan Project.

That day finally came on August 6, 1945. The day before, the crew had been briefed about their mission. Captain Parsons, who participated in the Manhattan Project, planning how the bomb would be delivered, had intended to show a film of the Trinity test, but the projector failed. Instead, he drew a picture of a mushroom cloud on the board and said the blast would destroy everything within three miles, and quite possibly the aircraft. He and Tibbets then instructed the crew to get some rest. Van Kirk played poker with his crewmates instead. "How they expected to tell you you were going out and dropping the first atomic bomb and it might blow up the airplane and go get some sleep, is absolutely beyond me," Van Kirk said in a video interview years later.

At Tinian Atoll, in the Mariana Islands, Colonel Paul Tibbets and his crew, including Ferebee and Van Kirk, took off in the *Enola Gay* at 2:45 A.M. Tinian time. Navigator Van Kirk sat behind Tibbets with his charts spread out on a table and his sextant in hand. He took bearings using the stars as a guide.

At 6:07, around sunrise, they rendezvoused with their escort B-29s over Iwo Jima and ascended to 31,000 feet. As they approached the target about three hours later, Van Kirk and Ferebee worked together confirming windspeeds and aimpoint, the T-shaped Aioi Bridge. At 8:15 A.M. Japan time (9:15 in Tinian), the planes were over Hiroshima, a city of 250,000 people, and the site of an important Japanese army headquarters.

"I got it," said Major Ferebee, seeing the bridge landmark in his site. Van Kirk leaned in and confirmed. He had guided the squadron to the target within a few seconds of its scheduled time over a six-and-a-half-hour flight. Ferebee then released the 9000-pound "Little Boy." The world would never be the same.

The uranium bomb began its 43-second descent to the city below. No one knew how strong the blast would be or if the crew would survive. Tibbetts immediately executed a diving turn to avoid the explosion. At 1,890 feet above the Aioi Bridge, the bomb detonated with the force of 20,000 tons of TNT, incinerating tens of thousands of Japanese instantly, and leveling a large section of the city. Countless thousands lie burnt and dying in the ruins.

On the *Enola Gay*, Van Kirk described what looked like a flash of light from a photographer's flashbulb engulfing the cabin, followed by buffeting from the blast's shockwave. Said Van Kirk years later, "The plane jumped and made a sound like sheet metal snapping. Shortly after the second (shock) wave, we turned to where we could look out and see the cloud, where the city of Hiroshima had been. The entire city was covered with smoke and dust and dirt. I describe it looking like a pot of black, boiling tar. You could see some fires burning on the edge of the city."

Van Kirk remembered feeling "a sense of relief." He later said, "Even though you were still up there in the air and no one else in the world knew what had happened, you just sort of had a sense that the war was over, or would be soon."

Turning back for Tinian, the squadron returned safely before 3 P.M. Van Kirk described the reception saying they were greeted by "more generals and admirals than I had ever seen in one place in my life."

Despite the dropping of millions of leaflets warning of the coming attacks and the subsequent devastation at Hiroshima, the Japanese did not immediately surrender. Three days later, the *Enola Gay* was back in the air as an escort on the Nagasaki mission, but Tibbets and his crew had done their part. Tibbets could have flown both missions but allowed others also to participate. The crew of *Bock's Car* had the honor of dropping the first plutonium bomb, "Fat Man." Finally, on August 15, Japan surrendered, ending World War II.

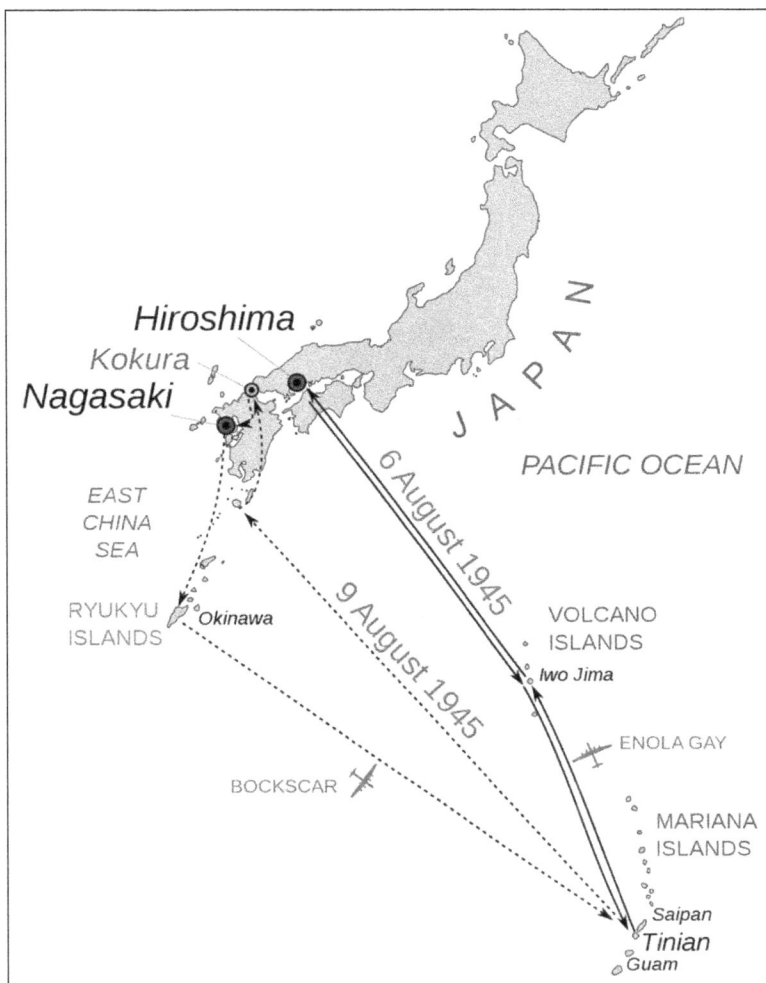

Van Kirk's course to Hiroshima and back

The Hiroshima bomb

Over the years, Van Kirk was often asked if, under the same circumstances, given a choice about the Hiroshima bombing, would he do it again? Said Van Kirk, "Under the same circumstances–and the keywords are 'the same circumstances' yes, I would do it again. We were in a war for five years. We were fighting an enemy that had a reputation for never surrendering, never accepting defeat. It's really hard to talk about morality and war in the same sentence. In a war, there are so many questionable things done. Where was the morality in the bombing of Coventry, or the bombing of Dresden, or the Bataan Death March, or the Rape of Nanking, or the bombing of Pearl Harbor? I believe that when you're in a war, a nation must have the courage to do what it must to win the war with a minimum loss of lives.

"You fight a war to win. There were over 100 numbered military targets within the city of Hiroshima. It wasn't a matter of going up there and dropping it on the city and killing people. It was destroying military targets in the city of Hiroshima—the most important of which was the army headquarters charged with the defense of Japan in the event of invasion. That had to be destroyed."

By the end of 1945, the Hiroshima bomb and its lingering effects killed approximately 140,000 Japanese, including 20,000 soldiers. Of roughly 76,000 buildings in the city, 92% were destroyed by the explosion and subsequent fires.

"It's too bad that there were so many casualties, but if you tell me how to fight a war without killing people, then I'm going to be the happiest man in the world," said Van Kirk.

Van Kirk received many medals and awards for his military service. Among them were his USAAF Navigator Badge, Silver Star, Distinguished Flying Cross, Air Medal with two silver and two bronze oak leaf clusters, Air Medal with bronze oak leaf cluster, Air Force Outstanding Unit Award with "V" device, American Defense Service Medal, American Campaign Medal, Asiatic-Pacific Campaign Medal with two bronze campaign stars, European-African-Middle Eastern Campaign Medal with two bronze campaign stars, and the World War II Victory Medal.

The text of the citation for the Silver Star awarded on September 22, 1945, for his role on the Hiroshima flight reads as follows:

Captain (Air Corps) Theodore J. Van Kirk, United States Army
Air Forces, for gallantry in action, while engaged in aerial flight
against the Japanese Empire on August 6, 1945. Captain Van
Kirk was Navigator for a combat crew of the B-29 aircraft of
the 393d Bombardment Squadron, 509th Composite Group,
20th Air Force, which flew from a base in the Marianas Islands
to drop on the city of Hiroshima, Japan, the first atomic bomb
to be used in warfare. Flying 1500 miles over open water to the
coast of Japan, they manned their assigned positions and crossed
the island of Shikoku and the Inland Sea. They constantly faced
the danger of being hit by anti-aircraft fire, enemy fighters, or
suffering mechanical or other failures, which would intensify the
risks of carrying this powerful missile. Throughout the mission,
the element of hazard from the unknown prevailed, for this was
the first time that this bomb, much more destructive than any
other in existence, had been dropped from an airplane. The
effect it would have on the airplane and these crew members
was only to be estimated. Shortly after 0900, they brought the
plane in over the city, and at 0915, the bomb release was pressed.
The bomb cleared and fell toward the planned objective. They
then headed from the area and, despite a minor effect from the
detonation, returned safely to their home base. By their courage
and skillful performance of duty achieved in outstanding fashion
despite the dangers involved in the accomplishment of this
historic mission, these individuals distinguished themselves by
extraordinary achievement and reflect great credit on themselves
and the Army Air Forces.

Van Kirk continued to serve after the war, participating in Operation
Crossroads during the summer of 1946 at Bikini Atoll, where atomic
bomb tests were conducted. He ended his service as a major in August
1946.

Van Kirk returned to college and received Bachelor and Master of
Science degrees in Chemical Engineering from Bucknell University in

The grave of Ted Van Kirk

1949 and 1950. He then spent the next 35 years in various technical and managerial positions with DuPont, primarily on the west coast.

Van Kirk and his wife, Mary Jane, had four children: sons Thomas and Larry, and daughters Vicki and Joanne. The couple was married until the death of Mary Jane in Hershey in 1975. She was only 51. Theodore then married Imogene Cumbie Guest of Stone Mountain, Georgia.

Van Kirk spent his retirement years appearing at universities, museums, air shows, gun shows, and on documentaries about World War II. In October 2007, he auctioned off his flight log he kept on board the *Enola Gay* during the Hiroshima mission. Van Kirk sold the log because he hoped a museum would acquire it. An unknown U.S. citizen purchased it for $358,500.

On November 20, 2012, Imogene Van Kirk passed away near Atlanta, Georgia. Theodore Van Kirk followed on July 28, 2014, dying peacefully with family members present. At 93, he was the last surviving member of the *Enola Gay* crew. Van Kirk was laid to rest at Riverview Cemetery in his native town of Northumberland, Pennsylvania, where he was a part-time resident.

28.

JOHN SIMON RITCHIE (SID VICIOUS)

AND

NANCY LAURA SPUNGEN

"The Sex Pistol and the Groupie (It's Better to Burn Out . . .)"

County: Bucks • Town: Bensalem
Buried at King David Memorial Park
3594 Bristol Road

It is a story that has it all: sex, drugs, and punk rock, if not rock and roll. You can also throw in a love story, a murder, and what some would call a murder mystery. The girl was born in Philadelphia, the boy in London, England. She was described by her teachers as "brilliant" and "intellectually gifted." His early school reports tell of a boy who was "bright, witty, intelligent but inconsistent in concentration." Her name was Nancy Spungen, and he was named John Simon Ritchie though the world came to know him as Sid Vicious and the pair as simply Sid and Nancy. She would die at age 20, and he would pass at the age of 21.

Spungen entered the world on February 27, 1958, in the City of Brotherly Love's University of Pennsylvania Hospital. Her arrival was not an easy one as she nearly died from oxygen deprivation after being choked by the umbilical cord during the delivery. It was determined that she suffered no ill effects from the experience and was released from the hospital eight days after her birth. Spungen was part of a well to do Jewish family that had a home in the Philadelphia suburbs. Her father was a salesman,

Nancy Spungen (left) and Sid Vicious (right)

and her mother operated a store called The Earth Shop, which marketed organic foods. Spungen proved to be so difficult a baby that she was prescribed barbiturates to calm her down. Her mother would later recall that she realized that it wasn't abnormal for babies to scream but that "Nancy did nothing but scream."

While these early episodes may have been indicators of emotional issues, she did well in school. At age five, she was rated as superior on an intelligence quotient test and was deemed qualified to skip a grade of elementary school. Socially she was unable to match her academic success. She made few friends and was inconsistent in dealing with her two younger siblings. She bullied and was sometimes violent in dealings with her sister but gentle and caring in her interactions with her brother. At the age of eleven, she was expelled from her public school because of a string of unexcused absences. Spungen would later run away from her private high school and attempt suicide. By the age of 15, her psychiatrist had diagnosed her to be schizophrenic. She managed to graduate from high school in 1974 and was accepted at the University of Colorado Boulder, which she attended for a little over five months. During her time at the university, she was arrested for buying marijuana from an undercover policeman and for having stolen property in her dorm room. She was expelled from college, and only through the intervention of her father was she able to arrange a plea bargain that resulted in her banishment from the state of Colorado.

She lived at home for a short time before moving to New York City at the age of 17. In New York, she worked as a stripper and became part of the alternative rock scene following bands like Aerosmith, the Ramones, and The New York Dolls. She became known as a groupie and had a short relationship with the Dolls' drummer, Jerry Nolan. She also began experimenting with heroin. When her relationship with Nolan ended, she headed to England following the band The Heartbreakers. Lee Childers, who served as The Heartbreakers' tour manager, wrote of Spungen, "She was a junkie, a drug supplier, and an all-around lowlife . . . She was a very, very, very, very, very, very bad influence on people who were already a mess. She was a troublemaker and a stirrer-upper." Shortly after arriving in London, she began exploring what was known as the "punk" lifestyle. It was during this period she pursued Johnny Rotten, the lead singer of the Sex Pistols, and met Sid Vicious.

The baby that the world would come to know as Sid Vicious was born on May 10, 1957. His parents parted ways soon after, and Vicious was mainly raised by his mother, Anne Beverly. At the age of three, Beverly took her son on a summer vacation to the Spanish island of Ibiza. The plan was that the father of her son, John Ritchie, would eventually join them and, in the meantime, would supply funds for their stay. Neither Ritchie nor the funds ever showed up. As a result, Vicious and his mother were dependent on the goodwill of those who had made their home on the island. The lad managed to make an impression on at least some of the residents. One of Beverly's friends told her, "Mark my words,

Anne, that child will either be the Prime Minister of England or a total dropout."

Eventually, both their own money and the charitable instincts of the residents dried up, so Beverly decided to return to England. After a short stay with Beverly's mother, the two found housing with an older woman who owned a home in Belham, a neighborhood in the south of London. Beverly went to work evenings and was able to leave Vicious in the care of her elderly landlady.

When Vicious began going to school, it became evident that, although he possessed the intellectual capacity to do the schoolwork, he had little interest in any subjects besides art and history. His reports from the Farm Street School reflect as much, but his time there was cut short after his mother married a man named Christopher Beverly in 1965, which required a move to Oxford. Six months after the wedding, the groom died from cancer, and mother and son were once again on their own.

The next few years saw Vicious attend multiple schools. When his primary and secondary education was completed, he found employment as a trainee cutter with a company called Daks Trousers. He was fired after making a mistake that ruined the pockets on hundreds of the apparel for which the company was named.

In 1973 he entered the Hackney College of Further Education to study art. It was at Hackney that he met a thin, long-haired Irish lad who would become his closest friend. The boy's name was John Lydon. In their book, *Sid's Way*, authors Keith Bateson and Alan Parker say that when Vicious encountered Lydon, he was meeting his "savior, champion, and eventual destroyer."

Lydon, who would become known as Johnny Rotten, was also involved in changing Sid's moniker. Lydon had a pet rat that he named Sidney. Vicious let him know that he was not very fond of that name, and as a result, Lydon began referring to his friend as Sid. He added Vicious as a last name because it was precisely the opposite of the Vicious personality. As Lydon later remembered, "Sid was one of the least vicious and least screwed up people that I'd ever met then or have met since."

The two friends began hanging around the shops located on King's Road in London. One day in the summer of 1975, Lydon was in one of the shops called Sex, a clothing store whose co-owner was Malcolm McLaren, the man who would one day manage the punk group Lydon would front. The young man stood out by dyeing his hair green and wearing a torn jacket held together by safety pins. It was here he met Paul Cook, Glen Matlock, and Steve Jones, all of whom were part-time employees in the store. These three invited Lydon to audition to become a part of their band. He must have impressed, for he became the lead singer of the punk group called The Sex Pistols.

In December of 1975, Vicious went to see his friend and his band perform. He thought they were terrific, and listening to the music, he felt an urge to dance. The main obstacle he faced was he had no idea how to do it. To compensate, he began jumping up and down while throwing about his arms. Vicious is thus credited with creating the punk dance that became known as the pogo, which within a year became an English craze enjoyed by many at every punk concert.

By 1977 The Sex Pistols were one of the best-known punk bands anywhere. The thing was that Glen Matlock, considered by many to be the most talented member of the group, was not fitting in. In hindsight, he may have been too serious a musician to get on with the other members of the band who appeared happy with drinking and partying their way through their life at the time. The reason given for removing Matlock was that he admitted to admiring The Beatles. Stating as much was apparently out of line for any Sex Pistol. At any rate, Matlock exited the group, and Sid Vicious became the bass player for the Sex Pistols. Vicious and his friend Johnny Rotten were already living together by this time, and Nancy Spungen had tried to strike up a relationship with Rotten, who had passed her off to Vicious. She may have been the happiest of all involved that Vicious was now a full-fledged member of the group. When it came to the new band member Manager McLaren would remark, "If Johnny Rotten is the voice of punk, then Vicious is the attitude."

Vicious had not picked the most convenient time to join the band. In an unprecedented move, EMI terminated their recording contract, although their initial effort titled *Anarchy in the UK* had been a hit. Also, because of the band's reputation and unpredictability, promoters were wary of booking them. None of this mattered to the band's new member who truth be told couldn't play the bass. Matlock, who didn't hold a grudge at the time, offered to give Vicious lessons to bring his playing up to speed. Vicious said he would call Matlock if he needed him. Matlock remembers, "He obviously thought he didn't because I never got that call."

Hooking on with Virgin Records, The Sex Pistols hit the studio to record an album which was titled *Never Mind the Bollocks, Here's the Sex Pistols.* Vicious missed many of the recording sessions because he was in the hospital suffering from hepatitis. This was most likely caused by his drug use, which had increased as his relationship with Spungen grew more intense. Vicious plays bass on just one song on the album.

The album itself created its own controversy. The two large chain stores, Woolworth and W.H. Smith, refused to carry the record. These two had so much influence that Virgin Records considered releasing the record after removing the song *God Save the Queen,* which was considered the most offensive. This idea was eventually dropped, but then a question was raised as to whether the word "bollocks" was obscene. Police all over England raided record shops and confiscated the album, saying it violated pornography laws. After a court case found otherwise, the record was a smash hit. Even without this publicity, Virgin had received 125,000 advance orders for the work, which meant that before release, it was both a number one and a gold record. This was a feat no band had achieved since The Beatles.

By 1978 it was clear that the band's days were numbered. A US tour lasted a little over a week due to multiple show cancellations. There was growing tension between Rotten, Vicious, and manager McLaren. To make matters worse, Vicious's heroin addiction was worsening. During one concert, he struck an audience member on the head with his bass. In Dallas suffering from withdrawal, he used a razor to carve the words "gimme a fix" on his chest before taking the stage. Those close to the group were convinced that Spungen was a bad influence on Vicious.

Rotten and McLaren even discussed kidnapping her to get her away from the bassist. The final concert took place at the Winterlands Ballroom in San Francisco. The band's performances were always hard to predict. On this occasion, Rotten was suffering from the flu, and Vicious fell over on stage multiple times. After 14 songs, Rotten said to the audience, "Ah-ha-ha ever got the feeling you've been cheated." That marked the end of the Pistols and the beginning of a solo career for Vicious with Spungen acting as a manager of sorts.

Vicious did not slide quietly into his career after the gig in Frisco. Leaving the scene of the concert, he was seen in a car with a group of girls who had rushed the stage during the show. A day later, he was in LA, partying on the Sunset Strip. Then he boarded a plane for New York chaperoned by one of the band's roadies. He was to fly from New York back to England, but after excessive drinking, he was taken from the New York airport and sent into detox. He insisted on being discharged after a few days and then reunited with Spungen before heading to Paris to film a sequence for a film *The Great Rock 'n' Roll Swindle,* which centered on the Sex Pistols and especially their manager McLaren.

Vicious plays a character in the movie called The Gimmick. In the film, he performs the song "My Way." Despite his dependence on drugs and what the director of the film, Julien Temple, viewed as a faked suicide attempt by Spungen aimed at delivering a message to her lover that he could never leave her alone, Vicious managed to make a positive impression talent-wise on the man charged with making the movie. Said Temple, "I believed that Sid, as a performer, had a unique possibility to present things that no one else could present. I thought he was tremendous. His performance on 'My Way' was great." For any interested reader, the performance can be viewed on YouTube.

In the spring of 1978, Vicious and Spungen returned to England. In an interview, he made a prediction. "I'll die before I'm very old. I don't know why. I just have this feeling. There are plenty of times when we've (he and Nancy) nearly died." After Vicious wrapped up work in London on the *Swindle* film, he and Spungen decided to move to New York City.

It is perhaps not surprising that the couple decided to live at the Chelsea Hotel, which had been home to the city's poets, beats, and drug abusers for years. Quite a few musicians had resided there as well, including Jim Morrison, Bob Dylan, Leonard Cohen, and Janis Joplin. The couple's drug dependency was evident in a filmed interview where Vicious extinguished his cigarette on Spungen, threw up, and slept while Spungen answered most of the questions.

Acting as his manager, Spungen was able to arrange performances for Vicious at Max's Kansas City and other clubs. One of these performances was taped and eventually released as the live album *Sid Sings*. Guitarist Steve Dior said that Vicious "got good money for these shows." The couple used the money to fund their heroin addiction, and these performances proved to be the last for Vicious.

Whatever happened in the couple's hotel room on October 12, 1978, remains unclear to this day. Around 10 A.M. on the morning of the 13th, Vicious called the front desk asking for help after finding Spungen dead on the bathroom floor, having bled to death after being stabbed in the stomach. The former Sex Pistol was found wandering the hallway in an agitated state and was arrested and charged with murder. After initially confessing to the crime, he recanted that confession and said he had been asleep when Spungen died. Some have put forth the theory that Spungen was killed during a drug deal gone wrong after Vicious had passed out from ingesting too many barbiturates. Malcolm McLaren believes that it was a botched double suicide—the thinking being that Spungen believed that Vicious had died from a drug overdose and then taken her own life. McLaren believed Vicious loved Spungen far too much to have murdered her. The young girl's devastated parents laid her to rest in King David Memorial Park in Bensalem, Pennsylvania.

After his arrest, Vicious was released on bail. He was rearrested after a bar fight in which the brother of singer Patti Smith was hospitalized after being cut in the face with broken glass. Once again, bail was arranged, and his mother, who was in New York, and friends decided to throw a party to celebrate his release. His mother scored drugs, and she was the one who discovered his body after he died from a heroin overdose on

The grave of Nancy Spungen, where the ashes of Sid Vicious were scattered

February 2, 1979. In 1996, his mother informed the journalist Alan G. Parker that she had administered the fatal dose because she feared that her son would be sent back to prison. She then had her son cremated and, against the wishes of the Spungen family, reportedly scattered his ashes over the grave of Nancy Spungen.

The couple is remembered in the 1986 film *Sid and Nancy* starring Gary Oldman and Chloe Webb. The movie was well received and has become a cult classic. In 2006, Vicious and the four original members of the Sex Pistols were inducted into the Rock and Roll Hall of Fame. The band refused to attend the induction ceremony.

216

29.

CONRAD WEISER

"Pennsylvania Peacemaker"

County: Berks • Town: Womelsdorf
Buried at Conrad Weiser Homestead
28 Weiser Drive

Johann Conrad Weiser, Jr., was the key interpreter and diplomat representing Pennsylvania and other colonies with the various Native American nations in the Mid-Atlantic region. Of German descent, Weiser emigrated in his youth with his family to New York and then to the Tulpehocken Valley in what is now Berks County, Pennsylvania. There, he put down roots and became an essential figure in the Pennsylvania Dutch community and a trusted emissary who was living on what was then the frontier. Many credit Weiser with maintaining peace with the natives during the early years of settlement and expansion in Pennsylvania.

Conrad Weiser was born November 2, 1696, the son of Johann Conrad Weiser, Sr., and his wife, Anna Magdalena. His father was a member of the Württemberg Blue Dragoons stationed at Affstätt in Herrenberg, in the Duchy of Württemberg (now part of Baden-Württemberg, Germany). It should be noted it was common among

Portrait of an elderly Conrad Weiser

Germans to assign the first name Johann or Johannes to all their sons, followed by the middle known by which they were known. This was certainly the case with Conrad and his father.

Not long after Conrad's birth, the elder Weiser was discharged from the Blue Dragoons and returned the family to Großaspach, a village about fifty miles to the northeast, on the opposite side of Stuttgart. Times were tough as the area continued to suffer from the previous religious wars. Then, in 1709, Weiser's mother died from a fever. Conrad, Sr., decided to seek better circumstances in the New World and joined thousands of other refugees from Germany, including many from the Palatinate. They traveled down the Rhine and then to London, England, where they stayed until the following year when Queen Anne arranged for transport to the New York colony. The plan was for the thousands of Germans, aboard ten ships, to settle on or around Livingston Manor, in the Hudson Valley of New York. They would be indentured servants, working the land until they had paid for their passage.

Not long after arriving, the elder Weiser settled his family in the Schoharie Valley, south of the Mohawk River. It was here, from 1712 to 1713, where young Conrad lived with the Mohawk and learned their language and customs. He returned to the German settlement, now known as Weiser's Dorf, and helped his father as a farmer. At age 24, in 1720, Conrad married Anna Eve Feck, the daughter of Johann Peter Feg and Anna Maria Risch. Anna was nine years younger than Conrad, only fifteen when the two married. Together, they eventually had fourteen children, seven of whom reached adulthood.

With the expansion of the German colony in the Hudson Valley, many became restless for new surroundings. In 1725, Conrad led a group of pioneers down the Susquehanna River and then east along the Blue Mountain to the Tulpehocken Valley, near what is now Womelsdorf, Berks County, Pennsylvania. This village happened to be along the Tulpehocken Path, used by the natives to travel from their villages up-river, especially Shamokin (modern-day Sunbury) to Philadelphia.

On or about 1731, Weiser met the Oneida chief Shikellamy, who was the regent at Shamokin, overseeing the settlement there. One legend says

Early photo of the Conrad Weiser house

the two met while Weiser was hunting. Regardless, it is likely the chief was passing near Weiser's home along the Tulpehocken Path. The two became fast friends, and Shikellamy suggested Weiser accompany him to Philadelphia to be his translator. Some had surmised the two might have met previously when Weiser was a youth in the Mohawk settlements and became reacquainted, but it was Weiser's knowledge of the language and customs that the chief valued. In Philadelphia, Weiser also impressed the governor and his council so much that he was hired the next year to be the interpreter at the conference in Philadelphia in 1732. The two then collaborated as ambassadors for the remainder of Shikellamy's life (until 1748), maintaining the peace despite tensions between the various tribes and the proprietors. (See the chapter on Shikellamy in this book for further details of their interactions and accomplishments.)

During these years, Weiser dealt with a personal spiritual crisis, moving his family to the Ephrata Cloister, in Lancaster County, to follow Conrad Beissel, a German preacher who had established a monastic order. After a few months, his wife returned to their homestead in Womelsdorf with the children. Conrad stayed on at Ephrata for six years but still managed to father four more children on his frequent visits home.

In 1745, Weiser's daughter Anna Eva met and married a young Lutheran preacher named Henry Muhlenberg. The two had three sons, one of whom was Frederick Muhlenberg, the future first Speaker of the House of the United States, and Peter Muhlenberg, a major general in Washington's army during the American Revolution. The elder Muhlenberg is regarded as the founder of Lutheranism in the United States.

After Shikellamy's passing, Weiser continued with his duties as the agent for the colonies. Later in 1748, he met in Logstown, in western Pennsylvania with chiefs from ten tribes. The French had been expanding in the area, and Weiser sought to maintain the friendship between the English colonies and the natives. Also that year, he planned the new town of Reading, east of Womelsdorf, on the Schuylkill River, and continued to be successful as a land speculator, merchant, and tanner.

By 1750, the loyalties of the natives were shifting. Weiser found during his visit to Onondaga that year, following the death of chief Canasatego, some of the Iroquois tribes were now favoring the French and were drifting away from the English.

Weiser's focus was now on the homestead. In 1752, he assisted with the creation of Berks County with Reading as its seat. Weiser was appointed the chief judge, a position he held until 1760. He was also a teacher and a lay minister of the Lutheran Church, and one of the founders of Trinity Church in Reading.

Two years later, in 1754, the colonies failed to hold a united front with the natives, who also could not agree. Each of the colonies set out to make agreements individually with the tribes. Weiser was able to obtain most of the remaining land of present-day Pennsylvania at this time, including areas still claimed by Virginia, in the southwest corner. It was George Washington's incursion into this area, on behalf of Virginia, that triggered the outbreak of the French and Indian War that year. Meanwhile, for his loyal service to the Penns, Weiser was granted a large tract of land on the Susquehanna River known as the Isle of Que.

With war waging in the western areas of the state, and raids occurring against frontier settlements, the government of Pennsylvania appointed Weiser and Ben Franklin to lead the construction of frontier forts. Weiser handled the areas to the west, while Franklin focused on the east. These forts helped defend the English settlements from incursions. Weiser served in the militia, leading the local troops defending Berks County.

In 1758, Weiser attended a council in Easton between colonial leaders and the Iroquois and other natives. Once again, Weiser's diplomacy helped to smooth over tensions, resulting in a treaty that ultimately led to the tribes abandoning the French. This resulted in the French demolishing Fort Duquesne and withdrawing from western Pennsylvania.

Monument honoring Weiser at the Conrad Weiser Homestead

Conrad Weiser died at Womelsdorf on July 13, 1760. He was buried on the grounds of his homestead. Following his death, relations between the natives and the colonies began a rapid decline. At the time of Weiser's passing, the natives of eastern Pennsylvania had mainly been united in the war against the French, and the war was virtually over in the commonwealth. But in the intervening years came Pontiac's War and the Paxton Boys incident, an event that would have been unlikely with a younger Weiser about. Over the subsequent years, the native peoples continued to be pushed west and north, and the commonwealth of Pennsylvania was mostly empty of them after the American Revolution. Looking back, it is apparent that Weiser helped oversee the peaceful transition of large portions of Pennsylvania from the aboriginal peoples to the English.

So, what if Conrad Weiser had not existed? Someone else would have likely come to the forefront. Perhaps George Croghan would have been the primary interpreter and negotiator. By all accounts, he was not as selfless and skilled as Weiser in this role, and it is likely the peace might not have been kept as long. What if, in the time of the Walking Purchase, the natives had risen and attacked Philadelphia? There certainly would have been a significant number of casualties, and the settlers coming to the New World would have been less likely to pick the Quaker colony and its vulnerable pacifist government. If Philadelphia was not as attractive a location, it would not have become the largest city in England's American colonies and is less likely to be the focal point for the many activities of the American Revolution.

Additionally, it is more likely the boundaries of Pennsylvania would be different, with incursions from Maryland in the south, Virginia in the west, Connecticut in the northeast, and the Canadian French from the north. Would Ben Franklin, who traveled with Weiser in the 1750s for some of the treaties, have risen to such importance if there was no peace with the natives and Philadelphia was a backwater town on a violent frontier? Without Franklin's pragmatism, would we have been able to unite thirteen disparate colonies into a new nation? Weiser did his duty on behalf of the colonial proprietors and died five years before the Stamp Act and fifteen before the battles at Lexington and Concord. Thus, we can never know what role an elder Weiser would have played in those times. We do know, however, the roles his progeny played in the next great act in American history.

Despite his contributions and his successful descendants, Conrad Weiser is a largely forgotten figure in American history, often overlooked and likely misunderstood. His Pennsylvania-German heritage was outside the mainstream of the politics and customs of the time, as was his lack of connection to the Quaker faith of his employers. His best advocates were those associated with the colonial governments, which were soon overthrown by a younger generation.

Conrad Weiser's homestead near Womelsdorf, Pennsylvania, is a National Historic Landmark administered by the Pennsylvania Historical and Museum Commission. There you can find his original stone house and his grave as well as those of many of his native friends. A monument to Weiser was erected there as well as a statue of his friend Shikellamy.

Nearby, the Conrad Weiser School District is based in Robesonia. Route 422 west of Reading on the way to Lebanon is named the Conrad Weiser Parkway. This road passes the high school and the homestead.

Camp Conrad Weiser is a 500-acre YMCA camp in Berks County. The Conrad Weiser State Forest is a tract of woodlands in upstate Pennsylvania.

The grave of Conrad Weiser

If you wish to try to connect with Conrad Weiser, we suggest a visit to his homestead. After spending a few hours understanding the essence of the man, drive the old Shamokin/Tulpehocken path north from Weiser's to Fort Hunter, Pilger Ruh, then to Pine Grove, then to Good Spring, then to Klingerstown, passing through Sacramento. Next, follow the back roads to Sunbury, the site of the former Indian village of Shamokin. There you can find the rock that contains a plaque memorializing his good friend Shikellamy on a busy street corner. Some say you can look across the Susquehanna near that point and see the profile of the Indian chief in the cliff face. While you will be disappointed with the sprawl of Sunbury, Pennsylvania, overtaking the once tranquil riverside native community, you will thoroughly enjoy the peaceful ride through the mountains. While in Sunbury, also check out the Northumberland County Historical Society for the native artifacts.

30.

AUGUST WILSON
"The Century Cycle"

County: Allegheny • Town: Pittsburgh
Buried at Greenwood Cemetery
321 Kittanning Pike

August Wilson was an American playwright who carved his signature on American theater by capturing the changing texture of black life in America in a series of ten plays, each covering a different decade of the twentieth century. The plays are known as the "Pittsburgh Cycle," also often referred to as his "Century Cycle."

When Wilson began writing his plays, he had little experience with theater, having only seen two plays, and having no formal training. Unencumbered by theatrical history, Wilson created his own rules for his plays. "I wanted to present the unique particulars of black American culture as the transformation of impulse and sensibility into codes of conduct and response, into cultural rituals that defined and celebrated ourselves as men and women of high purpose," Wilson said of his work. He did, and the skill with which he did it won him two Pulitzer Prizes, a Tony Award, and seven New York Drama Critics Circle Awards, in addition to twenty-three honorary degrees.

Wilson's rise from humble beginnings to Broadway was remarkable. He was born Frederick August Kittel on April 27, 1945, In the Hill District community of Pittsburgh. He was the son of Daisy Wilson, an African American cleaning woman, and Frederick Kittel, a German immigrant and baker who was mostly absent from Wilson's life. Daisy raised Wilson and his five siblings in a two-room, cold water apartment

August Wilson

above a grocery store at 1227 Bedford Avenue. It's been reported that Wilson's grandmother walked from Spear, North Carolina, where her family worked as sharecroppers, to Pittsburgh in search of a better life. Daisy managed to keep her children clothed and fed. When Daisy divorced Wilson's father and married David Bedford, the family moved to the white working-class neighborhood of Hazelwood, where they encountered a lot of racial hostility.

In 1959 Wilson entered Central Catholic High School, where he was the victim of constant race-based bullying and abuse. The next year he transferred to Connelly Trade School, where he felt unchallenged and transferred to Gladstone High School in Hazelwood. He quit Gladstone in 1960 after a teacher accused him of plagiarizing a twenty-page paper he wrote on Napoleon. He hid his decision from his mother and continued his education informally at the Carnegie Library of Pittsburgh, where he became a voracious reader. His extensive use of the Carnegie Library resulted in it later awarding him an honorary high school diploma.

By his late teens, Wilson had dedicated himself to the task of becoming a writer. His mother wanted him to become a lawyer and got fed up with him working at odd jobs and kicked him out of the house. He enlisted in the US Army for three years but somehow got himself discharged a year later. He moved into a boarding house at the age of twenty and began writing in bars, cafes, and a local cigar store. He wrote on paper bags, napkins, and yellow note pads and later typed them up at home.

Wilson officially erased his connection to his birth father when he adopted his mother's name in 1965. The symbolic starting point of Wilson's writing career came that same year when he purchased a used typewriter, paying for it with twenty dollars that his sister gave him for writing her a rush term paper on Robert Frost and Carl Sandberg. He decided he was a poet and submitted work to such magazines as *Harpers*. Although some of Wilson's poems were published in some small magazines over the next few years, he failed to achieve recognition as a poet.

In the late 1960s, Wilson joined a group of poets, educators, and artists who formed the Centre Avenue Poets Theater Workshop. Wilson met friend and collaborator Rob Penny through this group, and in 1968, they co-founded the Black Horizon Theater, a community-based theater company in the Hill District of Pittsburgh. It focused on politicizing the community and raising black consciousness. Black Horizons gave Wilson the chance to present his early plays, mostly in public schools and community centers.

In 1969 Wilson married Brenda Burton, a Muslim, and converted to Islam and had a daughter Sakina. He never fully embraced the religion, which contributed to the failure of the marriage, and they divorced in 1972.

In 1978 he went to St. Paul, Minnesota, to visit a friend, Claude Purdy, and decided to stay. Purdy helped him get a job writing educational scripts for the Science Museum of Minnesota and urged Wilson to write a play. In ten days of writing, while sitting in a fish and chips restaurant, Wilson finished a draft of *Jitney*, a play set in a gypsy-cab station. He submitted the play to the Minneapolis Playwrights Center and was awarded a $200 a month fellowship. The next year, in 1981, Wilson married Judy Oliver, a social worker, and quit the job at the museum to devote more time to writing. *Jitney* premiered at the Allegheny Repertory Theater in Pittsburgh and was accepted into the 1982 National Playwrights Conference. It became one of the Pittsburgh Cycle plays reflecting the 1970s.

Wilson's next break came when he met Lloyd Richards, artistic director and dean of the Yale Drama School. Wilson's play *Ma Rainey's Black Bottom* caught Richards' attention at a conference at the Eugene O'Neill Center in Waterford, Connecticut. Richards was the first black director of a Broadway play, *Raisin in the Sun* in 1959. *Ma Rainey* tapped into Wilson's interest in the Blues and its importance in American black history. Set in 1927, the play dealt with how black singers were exploited by whites. *Ma Rainey's Black Bottom* opened on Broadway at the Cort Theatre in 1984 with Lloyd Richards directing. It enjoyed a run of 276 performances and won the New York Drama Critics Circle Award for Best Play of the Year. Thus began a long collaboration between the seasoned director and the novice playwright. Richards went on to direct all of Wilson's plays and served as spokesperson and promoter for Wilson, who once described their relationship as that of a boxer and a trainer.

In 1987 Wilson struck gold with *Fences*. It opened on Broadway in March with James Earl Jones in the starring role. It ran for 525 performances and earned Wilson a Tony Award for Best Play as well as his first Pulitzer Prize for Drama.

Soon after *Fences* opened, Wilson added a second production on Broadway when *Joe Turner's Come and Gone* opened. It won the New York Drama Critic's Circle Award.

In 1990 *The Piano Lesson* opened on Broadway and won Wilson his fourth New York Drama Critic's Circle Award and his second Pulitzer Prize, becoming only the seventh playwright to win more than once. Also, that year Wilson divorced Judy Oliver and moved to Seattle. In

1994 Hallmark Hall of Fame produced a teleplay of *The Piano Lesson*, starring Charles Dutton and Alfred Woodard.

The successful runs on Broadway continued with *Two Trains Running* in 1992, *Seven Guitars* in 1996, *King Hedley II* in 1999, and *Gem of the Ocean* in 2004. *Two Trains Running* and *Seven Guitars* both won New York Drama Critic's Circle Awards, bringing his total to six, and when *Jitney* opened in New York in 2000, he was awarded his seventh.

In 1994 Wilson tried marriage again to costume designer Constanza Romero. The couple had a daughter Azula Carmen Wilson in 1997.

In 2005 *Radio Golf*, the last play in the Century or Pittsburgh Cycle premiered on April 22 at the Yale Repertory Theatre. Critics praised the play as a triumph, but discussion of the play was overshadowed in the press by public concern for Wilson's health, which had begun to decline. In June, he was diagnosed with liver cancer. On October 2, 2005, August Wilson died in a Seattle hospital. His funeral service was held at Soldiers and Sailors Memorial Hall in Pittsburgh, and he was buried in Greenwood Cemetery.

The American theater community publicly mourned his passing. On October 17, just two weeks after his death, the Virginia Theater on Broadway was renamed the August Wilson Theater in his honor. Also, in February 2006, the African American Cultural Center of Greater Pittsburgh officially became the August Wilson Center for African American Culture. In 2007, the Bedford Avenue home of his youth was declared a historic landmark by the state of Pennsylvania and placed on the National Register of Historic Places in 2013.

The *New York Times* wrote, "Heroic is not a word one uses often without embarrassment to describe a writer or playwright, but the diligence and ferocity of effort behind the creation of his body of work is really an epic story."

Wilson insisted he never wrote exclusively for blacks or whites, or any particular target audience. While one of his primary goals was to place African American culture front and center in a world where blacks had historically been forced to the social sidelines, he was perhaps most interested in taking a look at the human experience. Wilson knew any

August Wilson's grave

audience member of any color, could find some way to relate to the struggles and successes of his characters. Actor Denzel Washington, who starred in a 2010 revival of *Fences*, once noted that, though the events in Wilson's plays might appear to be specific to African American life, the overall themes are, in fact, universal.

Washington reprised his role in the 2016 film adaptation of *Fences*. He also produced and directed it. The film was nominated for four Oscars and won two Golden Globes. It was chosen as a top ten film of 2016 by the American Film Institute and grossed $64 million.

"I don't write particularly to effect social change," Wilson once said, "I believe writing can do that, but that's not why I write. I work as an artist. All art is political in the sense that it serves someone's politics."

BIBLIOGRAPHY

Books and Journals

Bailey, Pearl. *Between You and Me: A Heartfelt Memoir on Learning, Loving, and Living.* Thorndike, Me: Thorndike Press, 1990.

Bateson, Gregory Naven, and Margaret Mead. *Balinese Character.* New York: N.Y. Academy of Sciences, 1942.

Bateson, Keith, and Alan Parker. *Sid's Way: The Life and Death of Sid Vicious.* London: Omnibus, 1991.

Bernstein, Carl, and Bob Woodward. *All the President's Men.* New York: Simon & Schuster Paperbacks, 2014.

Callahan, Tom. *Arnie: The Life of Arnold Palmer.* New York: Harper, 2018.

Colonial Records of Pennsylvania, Volume VII.

Craig, Keith. *Herb Pennock: Baseball's Faultless Pitcher.* Lanham: Rowman & Littlefield, 2016.

Darr mine relief fund. Report to the Executive Committee Covering the Collection and Distribution of the Public Fund for the Dependents of the Men Killed by the Explosion in the Darr Mine of the Pittsburgh Coal Company, December 19th, 1907, 1910.

Davis, Ronald L. *Hollywood Beauty: Linda Darnell and the American Dream.* Norman: University of Oklahoma Press, 2001.

Dietz, Suzanne Simon, Theodore Jerome Van Kirk, Grace Snyder Van Kirk, D. M. Giangreco, and Richard Eugene Cole. *My True Course: Dutch Van Kirk, Northumberland to Hiroshima.* Youngstown, NY : Beau Designs, 2016.

Finafrock, John L. *Notes on Franklin County History.* Chambersburg, Pennsylvania: Kittochtinny Historical Society, 1942.

Frankfurter, Felix. "Mr. Justice Roberts." *University of Pennsylvania Law Revue* 104, no. 3 (December 1955): 311-317.

Fried, Stephen. *Thing of Beauty.* New York: Pocket Books, 1994.

Genovese, Vincent J. *Billy Heath: The Man Who Survived Custer's Last Stand.* Amherst, N.Y.: Prometheus Books, 2003.

Graeff, Arthur D. *Conrad Weiser, Pennsylvania Peacemaker, 2ⁿᵈ Edition.* Mechanicsburg, Pennsylvania: Sunbury Press, 2019.

Harder, Warren J. *Daniel Drawbaugh; The Edison of the Cumberland Valley.* Philadelphia: University of Pennsylvania Press, 1960.

Hougan, Jim. *Secret Agenda.* New York: Ballantine Books, 1985.

Knorr, Lawrence. *Gettysburg Eddie: The Story of Eddie Plank.* Mechanicsburg, Pennsylvania: Sunbury Press, 2018.

Lengel, Edward G. *General George Washington: A Military Life.* New York: Random House Trade Paperbacks, 2007.

Martin, Nicholas, and Jasper Rees. *Florence Foster Jenkins: The Inspiring True Story of the World's Worst Singer*. New York: St. Martin's Griffin, 2016.

McCallum, Jack, and Charles P. Bednarik. *Bednarik, Last of the Sixty-Minute Men*. Englewood Cliffs, N.J.: Prentice-Hall, 1977.

McCord, James W. *A Piece of Tape: The Watergate Story -- Fact and Fiction*. Rockville, Maryland: Washington Media Services, 1974.

Mead, Margaret. *Coming of Age in Samoa*. New York: Perennial, 2001.

————. *Growing Up in New Guinea*. New York: HarperCollins, 2001.

O'Sullivan, Shane. *Dirty Tricks: Nixon, Watergate, and the CIA*. New York: Hot Books, 2018.

Olson, Alison. "The Pamphlet War over the Paxton Boys." *The Pennsylvania Magazine of History and Biography* 123, no. 1/2 (1999): 31-55.

Pearson, Drew, and Robert S. Allen. *The Nine Old Men*. New York: Doubleday & Doran, 1937.

Pennsylvania Archives, Volume II.

Ritter, Lawrence S., and Donald Honig. *The 100 Greatest Baseball Players of All Time*. New York: Crown, 1986.

Sanger, Martha Frick Symington. *Henry Clay Frick: A Private Life*. New York: Abbeville Press Publishers, 1998.

Scavullo, Francesco. *Scavullo Women*. New York: Harper & Row, 1982.

Sipe, Chester Hale. *The Indian chiefs of Pennsylvania*. Lewisburg, Pennsylvania: Wennawoods, 1971.

Skrabec, Quentin R. *H.J. Heinz: A Biography*. Jefferson, N.C.: McFarland & Co, 2009.

Taylor, Frederick Winslow. *The Principles of Scientific Management*. New York: Harper, 1911.

Walsh, Tim. *The Playmakers: Amazing Origins of Timeless Toys*. Sarasota, Fla: Keys Pub, 2004.

Films

Florence Foster Jenkins. Directed by Stephen Frears. London: BBC Films, 2016.

Honest Man: The Life of R. Budd Dwyer. Directed by Jim Dirschberger. Harrisburg: Eighty Four Films, LLC, 2010.

Sid and Nancy. Directed by Alex Cox. London: Palace Pictures, 1986.

The Day the Bomb Dropped. Directed by Leslie Woodhead. New York: Smithsonian Channel, 2015.

The Food that Built America: Lines in the Sand. Directed by Nick White. New York: History Channel, 2019.

The Great Rock 'n' Roll Swindle. Directed by Julien Temple. London: Virgin Films, 1980.

Online Resources:

AfterAction.MilitaryTimes.com – for military sports information.
Ancestry.com – Family tree information and vital records.
August-Wilson-Theatre.com – for information about the playwright.
Brittanica.com – for information on many individuals.
BroadcastPioneers.com – for information about Philadelphia broadcasters.
CenterTheatreGroup.org – for information about August Wilson.
CoalandCoke.blogspot.com – for mining history.
CSMonitor.com – for information on many individuals.
Encyclopedia.com – for information on many individuals.
ExplorePAHistory.com – for information on many individuals.
FamousAmericans.net – for information on many individuals.
FindaGrave.com – for burial information, vital statistics, and obituaries.
IMDB.com – for information about movie stars and movies.
Inquirer.com – for Philadelphia history.
JosephPriestleyHouse.org – for information about Priestley.
Legacy.com – for recent obituaries.
Newspapers.com – Hundreds of newspaper articles were accessed—too numerous to
    mention here.
NYTimes.com – for New York history.
PhiladelphiaEncyclopedia.org – for information about Philadelphia.
PhiladelphiaMusicAlliance.org – for Philadelphia musical history.
PhilliesNation.com – Philadelphia Phillies information.
TeachingAmericanHistory.com – for information on many individuals.
TheHistoryJunkie.com – for information on many individuals.
TheReadOptional.com – for football information.
TVOverMind.com – for television news.
USAToday.com – for recent news stories.
USHistory.org – for information on many individuals.
USMineDisasters.miningquiz.com – for mining history.
Wikipedia.com – for general historical information.

Other Sources:

Joe Farley telephone interview with Mark Singel, June 2020.

INDEX

Charlotte Hornets, 149
Checker, Chubby, 153
Chelsea Hotel, 215
Chelsea Stadium, 144
Cherry Hills Country Club, 135
Chester, 153
Chester County, 3, 32, 39, 141, 174, 181
Chicago, Illinois, 39, 85, 98, 125–126, 128
Chicago Cubs, 148
Chicago White Sox, 143
Childers, Lee, 210
Childs, Adelaide Howard, 80, 84–85
China, 118
Chinchar, Barbara, 48
Church of England, 160
Churchill, Winston, 45
Cincinnati, Ohio, 89, 98
Circle, Taylor, 48
Clark, Clarence, 193
Clark, Dick, 153
Clark, Edward, 192
Clark, Mark, 199
Clean Air Act of 1963, 50
Cleveland, Ohio, 133, 153
Coal and Iron Police, 88–89, 93
Cobb, Ty, 143
Cochran, Elenore, 74
Coconut Grove Playhouse, 38
Cohen, Leonard, 215
Colbert, Claudette, 34
Collins, Charles, 63
Collins, Eddie, II, 148–150
Collins, Eddie, III, 148
Colorado, 210
Columbia Records, 5
Columbia University, 120, 122, 178
Committee for the Re-election of the President (CREEP), 116, 118
Como, Perry, 6

Computer Technology Associates (CTA), 60–63, 66
Concord, Massachusetts, 222
Conestoga (Indians), 67–69
Connecticut, 222
Connellsville, 124
Connelly Trade School, 226
Conrad Weiser Homestead, 187, 217, 219, 221–224
Conrad Weiser Parkway, 223
Conrad Weiser School District, 223
Conrad Weiser State Forest, 223
Cook, Paul, 212
Cook County Hospital, 39
Cooke, Jay, 98
Coolidge, Calvin, 174, 177
Coombs, Jack, 143
Cooper, Wilhelmina Behmenburg, 27–29
Coopersburg, 8
Coveleski, Stan, 146
Coventry, England, 205
Craig, Keith, 150
Crawford County, 59
Cressman, Luther, 120–121
Criswell, Benjamin, 94
Croghan, George, 17, 222
Cronin, Joe, 149
Crook, George, 90
Cullen, Frank, 170
Cumberland, Maryland, 20
Cumberland County, 51, 58
Cummings, Candy, 151
Cunningham, John, 48
Cunningham, Susan King, 70
Curtis Institute of Music, 152
Custer, George Armstrong, 13, 87, 90–91, 93

Dakota, Territory, 89
Daks Trousers, 211
Dallas, Texas, 32–33, 115, 213
Dallas Little Theater, 33
Darnell, Calvin Roy, 32

Darnell, Linda (Monetta Eloyse), 32–39
Darnell, Monte, 36
Darr, William, 54
Darr Mine, 40–44
Daventry, England, 160–161
Davis, Richard S., 110
Davis, Russell, 46
Davis Jr., Sammy, 5
Dean brothers, 67, 72
Dean, John, 117
Delaware (county), 152
Delaware (town), 133
Delaware (tribe), 67, 70, 182, 186
Democratic National Committee, 112, 116
Denver, Colorado, 98, 135
DePauw University, 119
Detrich, David, 74
Detroit, Michigan, 133, 153
Detroit Tigers, 143
Dewey, Thomas E., 45
Dickey, Bill, 146
Dickinson College, 165
Dior, Steve, 215
Directorio Revolucionario Estudiantil (DRE), 114
DiSanza, Bernardo, 48
Dissenting Academy, 160
Dolbear, Amos, 51, 55
Donora, 45, 47, 50
Donora Smog, 45–50
Donora Smog Museum, 50
Donora Zinc Works, 45–47, 49
Dorincz, Michael, 48
Douglassville, 116, 118, 173
Dovells, The, 153
Doylestown, 119
Drawbaugh, Bella, 54
Drawbaugh, Catherine, 52
Drawbaugh, Charles, 54
Drawbaugh, Daniel, 51–58
Drawbaugh, Elizabeth, 51
Drawbaugh, Emma, 54
Drawbaugh, George, 52